Magenta Fleurs

By

Caroline Clemens

Available through Ingram Sparks.

ISBN: # 978-0-578-90698-0

Published in 2021 by The Ivory Tide Press for Caroline Clemens under Pearl Media.

Book cover credit to Adrian Pasarin from adrian.dsgns on Instagram.

Copyright protected. This is a work of fiction, any similarities of characters are used fictitiously and the creative imagination of the author.

Find Caroline Clemens @ carolineclemens.com or theivorytide.com Caroline Clemens is the pen for Kim Troike.

Dedicated to three people:

Dave Thomas (I wanted to enter his book contest way back in 2001 but didn't know how to write),

Anonymous young patient who forever touched me as an ICU nurse and

Rose McGowan, who has inspired girls to be brave in the throes of adversity from bullies.

Thank you!

Magenta Fleurs

By Caroline Clemens

Chapter 1. Magenta Blood August 2020

"MAGENTA BLOOD by Chloe Clemons

If status is normal then what am I?
I go slow then fast, travel down then high.
They build rides for joy, funerals to sigh!
Kid's Legos are a toy, adults 39, the big lie.

Magenta is the color of the night
When all is soft, calm, and right,
The body is delivered, painless and free.
With a zillion stars outside peeking in
Peacefully I lay quiet without sin.

I have water, air, glucose, and cells,
Scientist and doctor perform miracles.
You left I stayed, you died I prayed.
My magenta blood sheds no tears
After exchanges gone are the fears!

"What, you say, are you saying?"
They buy me flowers and do the praying.
Because my heart has kept beating for two
My tears are joy yet we keep meeting.

Grandma's wisdom with praying tone
"Magenta blood delivers no sympathies!
You must eat those carrots and peas.
You'll get over it and will get along
Maybe you'll even sing a song."

I lay there breathing soundless at night
Purple dreams of majestic mountain sight.
No tears of loss remembering you my love
Days beat with life soaring high like the dove.
While bedside magenta fleurs petals drop tears.
I'm back to circulating red and blue with hidden fears."

    A moment of exhilaration relaxed Kristan knowing the reading was finished. If only the class knew the trauma involved for which her mother wrote the poem. She walked back to her seat looking over at a familiar face for assurance that she didn't blow it. Confident English teachers and now, professors in college, sometimes did this to the young and innocent. Teachers be damned. She tried to envision something that would make them explode inside, if only for a few minutes in front of hundreds. She smiled. What a thought. Her inward voice always managed to save her from the world. That or the cartoons she watched as a youngster had constant explosions in them. She'd watched boy gamers always shooting up the foe. Pow. Must be the poem about blood that brought this up. Maybe cause she was there with her mother the night of the explosive accident. Possibly the man in charge should just trip and fall.

Kristan sat down and straightened the papers together. Then she rested them on her desk. Kristan wore her blonde hair in a mid-length, straight cut which is kind of like her personality, straight up sweetness spilling like honey on a biscuit. Fit like a work out queen and the almost perfect southern girl, she wore a fashionable short skirt and tight top to class and yes, her makeup was on with cat eyes expressed for flair. Kristan could walk across a stage and own it. She had bravery and a can do attitude. She'd make a good friend, she just had to find some first. She finally looked up and noticed everyone was staring at her. Someone started clapping and others joined in. She sat there stoned faced as one single tear came down her right cheek. She waited for the professor. He came by and picked up her papers, then walked to the front of the class.

"Well done, Kristan."

Well, maybe he would change her mind. Well done echoed repeatedly. It crossed her mind that she watched too many cartoons as a youngster focusing on their explosions. The professor was wearing all black today. She wondered if that was for effect since her poem was picked from the pile of death poems. The other two subjects were unknown at this time and two other students would face her exact fate. Lucky her, she was done!

Professor Knox was well into his seventies with salt and pepper hair styled and cut, navy like, and seemed to love what he was doing. Smartly dressed, fit like a fiddle with a vested suite, long shirt and trousers, one wondered if he was a Shakespearean thespian in his younger day. The class would never know everything about this man-he had plenty to hide and he did so exclusively. He'd been married four times, so love was not his best resume. Maybe he just hadn't found the one yet, he surmised. He just couldn't give up the ship. So he worked on his students and tried to remember what it was like many moons ago to be young and in love. He was secretly very wealthy having inherited over 5 million dollars a while back. He was working on his place of retirement and still wanted to find someone to share it with. He quit smoking and took up vaping, where he can do it anywhere. His latest adventure was traveling to Spain. And next summer he planned on visiting England where he'd talk to his agent and publisher. But he wanted to take someone with him and share all that he had to offer. He looked around in search of a want. One never knew maybe he'd get lucky and meet a bright young student. Maybe. Or maybe their parent. He laughed at himself.

"Tomorrow's assignment is to bring in a hand written short synopsis of Kristan's poem. Two to three paragraphs are sufficient, and please, have no discussions with her about the poem. I want your thoughts before we find out the circumstances, if any. Tonight select one sonnet and one play to read from Shakespeare for the duration of this semester. Be prepared for tomorrow. Class dismissed."

Kristan texted her mom.

Thanks for the poem.

Chloe responded.

Ur welcome!

Kristan added.

Wonder if they have a clue?

Chloe

Likely not. You remember the story?

Kristan ended

Yes. You coming for parent's weekend?

Chloe smiled.

Wouldn't miss-see you then.

Kristan. <3 (heart)

Here she was walking across campus in the August heat. At last her hopes and dreams of becoming a nurse were set in place. That was the idea anyway but she felt lost. She wanted something and she didn't know what that was. Was this all there is: classes, dorms, and tests?

Vista University sure was beautiful with large live oak trees and the swaying moss catching the drifting winds, definitely different from North Georgia where it was quite windy blowing over her parent's glass tabletop twice while growing up. Her whole life lately had been consumed with graduating high school and getting into college. Now what? She strolled towards the cafeteria and lounge café. She needed a cool drink. She needed a friend at this massive university. She was happy she signed up for the sorority but they didn't start up until the second week of school. For now she was on her own.

Without warning a guy from her class began walking next to her.

"Hello."

"Hi."

"You headed for the café lounge?"

"I am."

"Can I join you?"

"Certainly. I do need some company."

"I know. It feels kind of strange to be out of high school and plunged into the big unknown."

"Yes. Not sure I want to be here."

"My older brother said it takes about a month or two before everything falls in place."

"You mean like getting used to being away from home?"

"I'm Jeremy. Let me be your friend."

"I'm Kristan. Let's go figure out what sonnet and play to choose."

The two smiled as Jeremy held the door open for Kristan.

The couple sipped iced lemonade then googled Shakespeare on their phones. Jeremy Moreau was French and inquisitive. He had that twinkle in his eye but didn't come on to a girl in a way that he possibly could, at this age anyway. He was slender, pale and had wavy dark hair. He loved to talk, therefore, he found girls pretty attractive and talkative. He loved exploring their minds and just maybe he'd get a chance to do more as a freshman away from his mother. He wore black boots and a belt with a chain attached. He almost looked like a biker. One wondered if he had a tattoo or when he'd get one and what would it be of. He was the baby of the family and all his siblings were married. He felt like he was on his own. Maybe this made him worldlier. His mother was single and lonely. She really needed to find a mate and leave him alone.

"I'm going to pick Romeo and Juliet as my play and Sonnet 116 about the marriage of true minds," said Jeremy rather hastily. Kristan couldn't believe he picked rather quickly. She studied the info before trying to find a title.

"I'll take Sonnet 18 about a summer's day and my play will be A Midsummer Night's Dream!" She exclaimed and once again, felt relieved. She picked based on summer as her favorite season and a dream felt like an escape. "I feel like we should go to a play or something."

"Quite funny. I picked love and you picked a season. We're both doomed." Jeremy seemed puzzled. They laughed and decided to go to dinner.

Later that night Kristan sat at her desk slumped over her homework. It was her poem which gave her an advantage. She prepared the story behind the poem and wondered what the professor was going to have them do with these poems after they were read aloud. He had told them three poems would be selected at random about three different subjects: death, ocean, and kids.

She skimmed through her Instagram and liked a few photos. Classmates were all over Georgia showcasing their dorm rooms with new friends in group photos. Some were out and about on the streets, and a few were down in the gulf for one last beach hurrah. Doubts crept in. It felt terrible to be a freshman again. She didn't get her feelings but she better get on it real soon. Could she be homesick already? She stretched out on her hard rock bed.

"Oh brother." She already missed home. She turned over on her side and cried to the wall. Loneliness shot through her like a hot glue gun mess. Then around eleven thirty her phone rang her favorite tune. It was him, Noah, her boyfriend from back home. She'd almost forgotten him. She was trying to. Noah wanted to get into the air force and had been trying diligently to make the bar which was set very high. Circumstances this year made for a later selection date. He complied. He already wore his hair short and worked out as much as possible. He was focused on himself but the two of them had dated and made a nice looking couple. He said he was going to come visit and take her to the beach for a weekend. Did she think that was a good idea? She said yes. Why did she say yes? She was at college now starting a new life. Say no. Call him back. But she couldn't do it. She decided to tell him at the beach-it would be their ending. What a cool way to say goodbye. Goodnight she told him.

Streaming sunshine woke her up like the alarm clock should have. She forgot to set her phone. Too many new things. Set it right now for tomorrow. And so she did. The window panes crossed right through the building across the parking lot. It was the library and she needed to go there after classes today. The pines were tall, spread out, and there were palm trees and palmettos too.

Someone knocked on her door. She opened it to find a girl named Lyndsay from down the hall.

"Hey, how ya doin?" Lyndsay asked.

"I'm doing okay. How about you?" Kristan returned.

"There's a party I heard about. It's tonight. I got a friend coming and we can all drive to it if you'd like to go."

"Sure. Is it a college party or what?"

"Oh, hell yes. It's a mixture but over by the fraternity houses. Let's go about nine."

"Can I invite a friend?" Kristan asked.

"Perfect. Nine o'clock, party mood!" Lyndsay left with a thumb's up signal. She was just another college girl trying to hook up and make a connection.

Kristan high fived her. Her first party besides the pledge parties that would happen next week. Rock on. She smiled.

Now she really had a reason to hit the library as soon as class finished. She waved bye, shut her door-and then posted a few Instagram photos of her room. Her little prison she thought. She was going to escape. She laughed and realized this thought was rather cynical, evil maybe. She should feel like the luckiest girl alive. But she missed home, her big beautiful home. Most of all she missed her mother. They were always close but now they had to separate. She had to: grow up, be with kids her own age, make friends, fall in love, get pregnant, get a degree, maybe get married, get a great job or career. Wait a minute … her mother would disapprove. She said: go to college, get a degree, get a job, meet someone, fall in love, get married, and later have kids. Oh yeah, travel is in there somewhere. Thinking about her mom put her in a good mood. There was a plan, just follow the plan she told herself.

Jeremy and Kristan sat in the back seat while Lyndsay and her hometown boyfriend, at least that's what she said, sat up front. Lyndsay drove while the boyfriend seemed to be high talking nonstop about whatever. He also put Lyndsay in her place constantly telling her how to drive and asking why they couldn't go to a friend's house first. Once there they mingled and headed for the big punch bowl. The music was loud and the place was wall to wall bodies.

Kristan looked for familiar faces. She was glad she brought her new friend.

As time went by she hadn't seen Lyndsay for a couple hours. She wondered had they left? Maybe she and Jeremy would have to find a ride home. He asked her to dance and she joined him. Feeling relaxed Kristan moved to the music. Talk about freedom. Man there wasn't any adults around. She contemplated if this was a good thing or not a good thing. She would have to be more grown up than she actually wanted to be. Someone put a headband around the top of her head hippie style. It went well with the short jean skirt and bolo top, not to mention the laced up flat leather sandals on her feet and calves. Around one in the morning Jeremy said, "Hey, let's get a ride. We got Dr. Knox early tomorrow and it's all about you."

"You are so right. I'm prepared. I just need some sleep."

Kristan went to sleep quickly but that wouldn't last. She found herself tossing and turning dreaming about last spring right before graduation. It had been stressful and this left her anxious. Why was she thinking about this now? She wanted to leave senior year behind her and embrace this brand new life. Everyone likely misses their parents and the little town they left behind. She would be going home for a weekend, and, of course, Thanksgiving and Christmas breaks.

She woke and sat up in bed. Maybe she had a case of the nerves. It was difficult saying goodbye to her mom and stepfather. But she quickly recovered on the walk back to the dorm room. Her mother had especially liked the garden outside her dorm room. She smiled. She would never know how much anguish this goodbye was for her because her mother hugged her strongly, so close; she didn't think she was going to let go. When she finally did-she gazed at her sorrowfully, and then touched Kristan's cheek and the heart of her lips. Then they turned to leave waving goodbye and headed for the car. Kristan turned and walked back to the room smiling and filled with pleasant thoughts. Everything was too exciting to be wrapped up in missing anyone as yet. This was her life. She was in college and looking for friends. She got out of bed and went to the bathroom in her single bed dorm room with a bathroom inside. The night was still and she guessed it to be around three am.

She came back to her room and made sure she had her phone alarm on. When Kristan passed the mirror in her room she didn't recognize the girl in front of her. Maybe she was leaving everything behind and transforming into a new person. She took out a single dose white wine from her fridge and sipped it. Maybe this would help her fall asleep.

Chapter 2. Fort Knox

Kristan left early for class and did not see any other girls in the hall. She put last night out of her mind and walked to class. Once she sat down she looked around and there was Jeremy a few rows over. She nodded and they acknowledged each other. A familiar face-that's exactly what she needed.

Her phone dinged and without looking she turned it off. She didn't need any interruptions, not today. She had to tell the story behind the poem. She needed to sound confident and calm.

Professor Knox took the roll call for attendance. He wanted to know their names and placement in the room more than anything else. This was the first week of class and he wanted to know who is in it to win it. He looked at their facial expressions when called upon.

Enthusiasm.

Timeliness.

Attentiveness.

Literature appealed to the heart and mind, the more you knew the more you wanted to know. He wanted his students to feel the rhythm of their own soul, learn some Shakespeare, practice poetic structure, and write what inspired them. By choosing a topic from the selection of three he would know where their inspiration lies. He thought maybe he could help them to appreciate others by knowing their world, and what was important to another human being through literature if possible. This sounded noble and ancient, he realized, but he was from the flower power mad 60's era and would be retiring very soon. He'd purchased ten acres in the mountains near a small lake and planned to write a novel, maybe two. He'd sold poems to foreign magazines and culture outlets but he wanted to write the great American novel and go beyond the dead poet's society. He even had a publisher, yes, one of the big five wanted him. For years they offered him six figures to write. He was ready now. He better get to it before they pulled back. Next year at this time that's where he'd be. Lucky him. The idea for his novel would involve the winner, or outstanding poem from this class he had decided. He smiled. How cunning. Of course, he would ask the author if he could use the selected poem and write it into a Shakespearean sonnet. He would include their name as well inside as a coauthor.

Today he was dressed in his Parisian clothes: black pants, laced up leather black boots and a frilly sleeved, flouncy white shirt with no tie but a satchel of material at his throat. He looked like the painter Dali minus the mustache. He did this purposefully to intimidate, authenticate and frustrate the student to reveal the emotions behind the poem. Oh, and to have a few laughs as well. Especially with the morbidity of the subject today he figured everyone could look at him, wonder, and let out a laugh. He nodded to Kristan-she saw his outfit and her eyes grew big and staring.

"Kristan Lindemann."

"Present," she stated. She didn't smile or stop her staring. He too engaged her eyes for a while. He knew she was serious about the nature of her learning and what she might understand from the lesson. He paused. Enough for Jeremy to take note and wonder.

What's up he thought?

Jeremy coughed to break the silence. Professor Knox looked back at his computer for the next name. "Jeremy Moreau," said the professor.

"Here."

"How are you Jeremy?" asked Professor Knox.

"Not as good as yesterday but better than tomorrow." He thought that sounded confusing.

"Trending down."

Anyone not paying attention missed that trend. Professor Knox knew Jeremy to be of quick wit. He liked that. He could play that game for sure. He smiled with closed lips at Jeremy.

Kristan and Jeremy exchanged glances. For then the two of them relaxed and thoughts arose about if they would see each other tonight. And are they just friends or is there something to be explored? Kristan had no idea. Jeremy thought she was beautiful-so, yes, if it happened. Why not his older brother used to say.

"Before Kristan begins to tell the story everyone bring up your three paragraph analysis of her mother's poem and drop them in the basket."

When everyone had returned to their seats the professor had Kristan rise up to the podium. He asked her if she was ready and she replied, "Yes, I am." He turned on his speaker and a YouTube mix came on. It was a Hauser Cello *Pas de Deaux* from The Nutcracker.

Kristan began, "In the city of Paris, back in 1996, my mother and her future husband were to be wed in a small ceremony at the Notre Dame Cathedral. My dad was the organist and director of music there. My mother Chloe was an artist. She was a painter. They met in a café-typical story of American meets Parisian. They wined and dined and fell in love! He wanted to move to America and had applied for a position with a symphony as a conductor. My mother says the wedding and reception were perfect. All good. On their way to the hotel there was a car chase and they tried to avoid it but crashed their vehicle. My father died at the scene while my mother was taken to the hospital. She nearly lost her life, it was touch and go. Her nurse's name was Marilyn and this lady saved her. It took months and months of recovery with all the broken bones, casts and surgeries. Dr. Liphart was her surgeon and had to come and tell her that her new husband was gone. This is the kind of news that could literally kill someone. We know that I was conceived the night before as my mother had heard brides are tired on their wedding night. She decided they should participate in that event early. I was floating around while she almost lost her life. My mother says this is the most horrific and dramatic story she has ever been involved in. She tries to paint through it. Thank you for listening."

Professor Knox turned off the music and walked around the class. This was quite a story. He didn't know what she was going to say but he knew it involved blood, death, and life. He knows his students are young, fresh out of high school, and are just beginning their lives and may not have experienced death quite like this. This is good. Emotions. Feelings. Pain. Death. Life. This is why he does this. He teaches his students to use literature, poetry, and real life to intersect. He likes to think his music brings the rhythm or heartbeat in for a stroke of artistic reality.

"Raise your hand if you'd like to say something."

The hands went up. He pointed to them to speak aloud.

"I'm so sorry Kristan."

"I'm sorry too. I've never known anyone who has died."

"I feel bad. You never got to meet your daddy."

"There she was in the most beautiful city and at her wedding."

"Everything stopped just like that."

The comments went on for a while then silence took over. Kristan looked at her phone wondering how soon class ended. She didn't mind the kind responses she just didn't really want to talk about it anymore if she didn't have to. She did not feel like crying. This was something she knew about her whole life. Maybe she should feel worse. Maybe she released the burden or buried it when they had his funeral at age eight when they flew to Paris one summer. They tossed his ashes in the ocean near a coastal town. What was the name of that town? Her grief was finished or so she thought.

"I heard that when one life ends another begins. My mom always repeats this when a relative of hers dies, or when she reads the obituaries and births in the paper."

Professor Knox added, "That might go with the soul's theory, one dying, and one being born or enlightened."

"Professor, I thought our soul is inside us, just for us."

"Good thought. Soul music, soul food. Someone Google it."

"Spiritual energy, music, or mortality."

Many things to consider here. Definitely it is something we cannot see. Today we are going to take a twenty minute break. See you at 10:40."

"Class we have some questions to ask. Don't we? First up is why the title of Magenta Blood?"

"Magenta is both red and blue, a mixture."

"Yes. It is."

"Makes sense coming from an artist."

"How do you think Dr. Liphart contributed to this poem?" he asked.

"Oh, I believe she helped Chloe to understand her condition of almost dying, not being alive nor dead."

"After all she likely came to see her every day, and the nurse cared for her many hours a day, day after day."

"And don't forget about the wounds or bleeding that Chloe might have seen creating memories of all the blood in the car from her new husband."

"She did call it the color, the color of the night, when all was calm."

"Possibly in the car when everything was stopped: no lights, no sounds, a deadness if you will, made her feel that way."

"I like that. Very good." Professor Knox was in agreement.

"She could probably see with her eyes but not move."

"To be or not to be," Professor Knox couldn't resist.

"She adds the sentiment of religion in there, too," one of her classmates adds.

"She most certainly does. With the ceremony and reception over they have not had the wedding night. Only Chloe knows this and later she will live with this forever. For some not a problem, but others could judge and this might weigh on her heart and cause distress."

"Ah ha, a tragedy in more ways than one."

"Then grandma who is older and wiser tells her no sympathies but to get on living by eating, breathing, and singing," Professor Knox said.

"The older folks, the grandparents, don't always talk about things that cause pain or distress. They just hide them and don't want all the truth out."

"Why is that do you think?"

"Because maybe they got into trouble or were caught in something they weren't supposed to be doing."

"I know they sing songs about dying like hymns."

"Church songs." Adds another classmate.

"The last stanza of the poem definitely is all Chloe, serenely, resolutely going forward eyeing the majestic mountain, purple in color, baby in womb, dying petals dropping and her own life back to red and blue."

The class members nodded in agreement. They could see it by feeling it. The decisions made decisive by a mother to be. What else could she do but go on, leaving the death to the petals on the table?

"I'll read your paragraphs tonight and tomorrow we begin with the next poem, one of the oceans. Sara see me after class. Taylor, please see me as well. Class dismissed."

Sara looked up. She guessed he liked her poem she submitted. She giggled. Good. Sara was a serious girl with an occasional giggle. She actually thought her English instructor, the professor was very hot. She loved how he came to class in different costumes if you will. This made him be on their level, all new and feeling awkward. Now she had a chance to speak with him on a one on one basis. This made her shiver and feel slightly excited.

Chapter 3. The Bean Dip

Kristan pledged a sorority the second week after classes began and had met a fellow pledge named Taylor. She and Taylor went to eat Mexican food one night at The Bean Dip. A couple of the upper classman and sorority gals joined them. This was going to be a party, Mexican hats and all. The fake ID's came out and the Tequila was poured. Lick the salt, shoot the tequila shot and suck on the lime. They would order food but first came the tequila with many laughs and sour faces. And then another round.

The waiter came by after the second round, "Are you ready to order food?"

"Hey, we are just getting going. Who's ready for a third?" Kristan asked her new friends and then looked at the waiter. "What's your name again?"

"Levi. I'm Levi. A pleasure to meet you." He shook her hand.

"I'm Kristan. This is Taylor, Sara, and Dana. You're cute!" Kristan said with too much glee. The girls giggled.

"Nice to meet all of you. Y'all must be students at Vista. I go there as well and work here part time." Levi had a big smile. Kristan thought she'd like to talk with him some more.

"When you get done working come sit with us, okay?" She asked.

"Certainly. I will do just that."

He took their food order and added a third shot of tequila all around. He was done after he served their food, and decided to join them. He ordered and served himself dinner too. Levi had wavy dirty blonde hair and he wore it on the long side. He sat down across from Kristan, in between Taylor and Dana. She noticed his ever-present smile and a laugh that didn't quit. In a few short minutes she noticed a spark between Taylor and Levi. Were they flirting with one another? Kristan thought as much.

Sure enough by the end of the evening the two of them were sharing social media and making a connection. Kristan would check in with her fellow pledge later on and get the scoop. She smiled. She also noticed that Levi noticed this smile.

What a great evening. College was proving to be fun, adventurous, and full of guys. The mariachi band played an extra song at their table allowing some side to side sway and loud singing. Arms were over each other's shoulders like old friends. She would definitely be returning to The Bean Dip!

The next morning Jeremy caught up with Kristan and walked her to class. They discussed what was ahead with Professor Knox. It would be enjoyable thought Kristan as the bulk of class time was off of her. Jeremy agreed. He hoped he didn't get picked but if he did he would be ready. He had selected the kid's topic for poetry. He could do kids because he had been a camp counselor for three years. He knew how they reacted, what they liked, and the way they talked. He wrote a poem about worms, rather night crawlers from a story a kid told him at camp.

"Let's stop and have breakfast before we go to class. You want some?"

"Yes. Great idea. I'd like an iced coffee this morning," Kristan craved a cold pick me up.

"Perfect." Jeremy held the door open for her. She thanked him and noticed how green his eyes were. Thus far she was meeting guys at college but they seemed like friends not possible boyfriends. She wondered about that for a while as she followed him over to the coffee section. Was it the studying, classes, or availability everywhere? Maybe it was the new place as she didn't feel settled. She still missed her mom, quite a lot, if she thought about it for too long. Possibly it's the focus on "I'm at college and this is for me!" Then again, she'd heard that in college people just hook up and it's not serious. Hmm. Kristan had no thoughts on that idea. Likely it just had to happen. Don't think about it. All of a sudden she heard extremely loud talking and quite a rumble over at the table full of very large muscular guys. She assumed it was the football players-they looked big and hungry as their plates were piled high. She took a sip of her iced mocha latte and when she sat it down a guy she had never seen before asked if he could sit with her.

"Sure."

"Thanks. Appreciate it."

"You're welcome."

"No breakfast?" he asked.

Just then Jeremy returned with two plates of food: eggs, waffles, and fruit.

"Hi. Jeremy." Jeremy stuck out his hand and the fellow did the same.

"Mike, great to meet you."

"You too."

"I'm Kristan, and my hands are icy cold. Nice to meet you."

This meeting of people seemed so easy, unlike high school where everyone stared or ignored you constantly. It was in that moment Kristan figured out she loved college. She smiled then laughed.

"Kristan, what is funny? Do I have spinach in my teeth?" Mike asked.

"No, not at all. I just love college. We get to meet so many people all day long. Everyone is friendly."

"Totally agree." Jeremy concluded.

"And it's only the third week. Think of how much fun and studying we get to do." Mike chided.

"I heard the studying gets to be more and more. Just think of how smart we'll be come spring." Kristan enjoyed her iced mocha latte and her brand new friends.

"Hey, y'all been downtown yet?"

"No, will our fake ID's work?"

"Well, there are a couple places with live bands. You should come and see them. One of my friends is the guitarist." Mike said.

"Sounds good. What time?" Kristan asked.

"The band starts at ten."

"Hey, we'll catch ya there this weekend."

"Sounds like a plan. I should ask Taylor and her new friend from The Bean Dip, Levi." Kristan said scheming.

Professor Knox appeared calm today and had shorts on. He took attendance but didn't look up like he usually does. Then he turned on the sea music, rolling waves hitting the shore. Kristan took a big gulp of her latte thinking she might fall asleep. She felt like if he caught you asleep that was an F.

"Does anyone know what The Tempest is?"

"Shakespeare play."

"Yes, that is correct. Written when?"

"Sixteen eleven."

"I see you have studied. Great. The sea becomes the plot or as a symbol of man's hope for a rebirth. Why is this?"

"Because it starts out tragic with a father and his daughter getting shipwrecked on an island for twelve years."

"True. We are not studying this play I wanted you to know that water was important to Shakespeare and how he played with it. Sara will read her poem about the sea, please note the author, and Taylor has a short poem to read as well. I liked both and wanted the class to hear them."

Professor Knox turned on more serious music like darkness on the sea hallowed out on an organ with large pipes in an old church. The class imagined.

Sara began ... "The Storm by Caroline Clemens

The Storm

Our direction in discord, we set upon mighty sea,
In search of Tilapia, sardines and fishes tail.
The storm and catastrophe, we men did not see,
As River Jordan broke free, the wind disturbed our sail.

Our fellowship soon tested, on this agitated lake.
Males sufficiently ruffled, when the line snapped that night.
It shall surely seize us, keep calm for Jesus sake!
Large swells beneath our boat, hands worked a tenacious fight.

The halcyon day became a passionate tale.
In Rembrandt's canvas, a space emits the light.
Christ's surveillance besets refuge within the rail.
Our fishing boat turns aside, capsize a certain site.

We obediently seek his word and find calm.
Not elite, gentry, nor lord or royal king,
Just peers reformed from dread, red blood rejoicing in psalm.
This carcass shall not flail, with lord aboard we sing!

Its severity and spirit, Oh! The sapphire night,
On an amethyst sea with bleached ivory swells,
When the tempest calms, peaceful, we wallow in this sight.
Christ's reverence for the sea, fish for many he yells."

The class was quiet. Professor Knox turned back to the lapping waves.

"Why did you pick this poem Sara?" asked Professor Knox.

"I enjoyed the religious aspect mixed with a Rembrandt painting, Christ, fishing, and the coming sapphire night intertwined with faith. To me it almost sounds romantic."

"It is about being saved, rejoicing, and psalms, or singing." he replied.

"Yes. Then the storm or tempest calms, like a plot, according to Shakespeare. I think it fits all the criteria." Sara spoke calmly and quietly.

"Taylor is going to lighten the mood with a very playful poem by her. Listen up."

"Paradise by Taylor

Paradise

Beneath the sea,
Frolics you and me.

If ever we are caught,
Such a battle will be fought.
The air is gold above the ivory tide;
Yet, free we glide in our coral and aqua ride."

Taylor went back to her seat. She loved this little poem of hers. One morning she wrote it out in only three minutes, maybe less. She liked to think this gave way to divine intervention. She laughed. Many in the class smiled at her.

"Perfect. Both excellent poems and uniquely different. One of strength, courage, and prayer, and the other of two fishes swimming in the sea without a care unless they are caught. Fine. Fine."

The class clapped for both of them. Professor Knox gave instructions.

"Please do your analysis on Sara's poem. Give me your version in three paragraphs. And Taylor's is fairly explanatory. Please explain why you think Taylor calls this Paradise and tell me about her form, noting the curve or placement of words on paper. Thank you both for your participation."

Kristan spent part of the evening working on this assignment. She wondered if her mother might want to hear this poem and give her an analysis. She called her and read her the poem. After she finished the line was quiet and both women paused, mother and daughter, registering the words. Her mother spoke first.

"Very good."

"I know, right."

"The class will have much to discuss tomorrow."

"Yeah, I think three paragraphs will be easy to write."

"You like this class I can tell." Her mother said the kindest things just when she needed them.

"I do. Can you believe it?"

Pause on both ends.

"Poetry is like a little song that you can see. I think that is it. Okay, I better go and write it up. And I have three other subjects to work on."

"We'll see you in October, sweetie."

"I'll face time you this Friday before the weekend."

"Okay, until then. Goodnight."

Kristan finished her homework then put her nightshirt on and retrieved a white wine out of her small fridge. She still had two small bottles left from the four a friend gave her the first week of college. She climbed up to her bed, laid down and felt a little dreamy tonight. Her nerves of being the new gal in unfamiliar territory were dissipating. The decision to break up with Noah came rather easily and she would do it after one last escapade. He was taking her to the beach to stay at his grandmother's unoccupied condo. She knew they would have a fabulous time playing on the beach, swimming in the ocean, and saying goodbye to each other. He hadn't heard from the Air Force or Naval Academy, as yet, but they assured him he was still in the running to attend for next year. Kristan was excited for him in that he would have his life and she would have her own. They both needed to live a little and not rush into marriage just because they'd been an item. Likely you couldn't even marry while at the academy anyway. She was doing him a favor. This made Kristan feel like an adult beyond her years.

Chapter 4. Magenta Fleurs

Kristan asked Jeremy to check out the restaurant Magenta Fleurs downtown telling him they could visit the band playing nearby. "I just need to check out this restaurant because I want to take my mother and father here when she comes for parent's weekend and I don't want it to be a dive or something."

"I understand Kristan that it being the same color as your mother's poem."

"Oh, I almost forgot, you're right. Then I especially need to make sure it's a fit. I trust Dr. Knox. I think."

As they strolled the downtown there was a sweet potion in the air. A soft warm August night in the coastal region of Georgia made it special. Music popped here and there with lingering notes of jazz periodically taking you farther away. To where Jeremy didn't know. He supposed it reminded him of Savannah when he took his date out on their senior prom night. Wake up Jeremy you're in college now he thought. Kristan looked pretty tonight like she didn't have a care and was more relaxed.

"There it is!" She pointed and they walked up to the front door to check out the menu. Silence. They met one another's eye and returned reading.

"It sounds fancy. But yummy." Jeremy relinquished.

"Perfect. My mother loves this type of food. The fancier-the better. And look it's all made to a southern beat. She will love me no matter what I do!"

Jeremy looked and laughed. "You need some bribery do ya?"

"What about us? Let's order an appetizer and sprite at the bar."

"Sure. Then we'll go listen to the band across the street and the other one a few blocks away."

"Let's review our sonnet and play choices. Shakespeare a la carte!" Kristan exclaimed.

"Lovely idea. Wow. Would anyone believe we are studying downtown in a fancy bar?"

"When we get A's in the class we'll tell them our secret," Kristan said believing studying could be fun, social, too.

Kristan had chosen sonnet 18 *Shall I Compare Thee to a Sunny Day?* and the play *A Midsummer Night's Dream*. Whereas Jeremy chose sonnet 116 *A Love Sonnet* and the play *Romeo and Juliet*. Kristan and Jeremy retrieved their sonnets via their cell phones. Kristan urged Jeremy to go first. They felt by reading them out loud both would find a comfort level and familiarity for later in class. "Go on I'm listening."

"Love Sonnet

Let me not to the marriage of true minds,

Admit impediments. Love is not love

Which alters when it alteration finds,

Or bends with the remover to remove:

O, no! It is an ever fixed mark,

That looks on tempests and is never shaken;

It is the star to every wandering bark,

Whose worths unknown, although his height be taken.

Loves not Times fool, though rosy lips and cheeks

Within his bending sickles compass come;

Love alters not with his brief hours and weeks,

But bear it out even to the edge of doom.

If this be error and upon me moved,

I never writ, nor no man ever loved.

By William Shakespeare"

"Bravo. Bravo." Kristan clapped with spirited enthusiasm. It was early and none were at the bar. Jeremy smiled. He was enjoying this studying out In the open. What a concept!

"Time's up. It's you."

"Shall I Compare Thee to a Summer's Day?

By William Shakespeare

Shall I compare thee to a summer's day?
Thou art more lovely and more temperate.

Rough winds do shake the darling buds of May,
And summer's lease hath all too short a date.

Sometime too hot the eye of heaven shines,
And often is his gold complexion dimmed;

And every fair from fair sometime declines,
By chance, or nature's charging course untrimmed;

But they eternal summer shall not fade,
Nor lose possession of that fair thou ow'st.

Nor shall death brag thou wand'rest in his shade,
When in eternal lines to Time thou grow'st.

So long as men can breathe, or eyes can see,

So long lives this, and this given life to thee."

"Mines longer but hey we did it." Kristan said.

"We should play a game and you read a line then I read a line and in between the other says what it means. The first thing that comes to mind-doesn't mean it's right or wrong. Just is."

"I do like that idea. Just is."

The couple who was studying at the bar in one of the finest restaurants near coastal Georgia took time to order an appetizer. Tonight's singer was warming up and they didn't mind the interruption. There's that feeling when two people bond and they both know it. That just happened. Just happened without knowing or trying, that is, the young couple experiencing downtown on a Wednesday night in August in the south.

When Jeremy and Kristan left the bar Jeremy thought he had experienced the best date ever and he had. Kristan thought the exact same thing. They walked to the next bar where the guy they'd met at the cafeteria said he was playing or a friend of his anyway. Jeremy held Kristan's hands up to his and kissed them. He looked her in the eyes and she him. After the kiss he said, "Kristan, I believe we just had the most perfect date. Let's not ruin it, let's stay friends."

"I feel the same way. Is that possible?" Jeremy was cute for sure. But somehow they cut across lines and their friendship seemed to be going deeper. He hugged her and then the two of them walked into a band party with big smiles on their faces.

They grabbed a table, set their phones down and joined a few others on the dance floor. What seemed like hours and hours of dancing but was actually two finally made them take a break. A couple girlfriends of hers had come too so Jeremy had time to sit a few songs out on the sidelines. The place got busier and busier. Jeremy went to get them waters while she went to the bathroom. Man, college was turning out to be fun thought Kristan. She fixed her makeup and brushed her hair after all that dancing. She returned to the table but no one was there. She saw two waters and picked one up gulping about half of the drink. That's when she heard Jeremy say "I'll get the drinks."

Drinks. Well what were these? Damn she was at the wrong table. Oh no. Quickly, she made her way over to the right table. Oh well, she thought. She shook her head back and forth like she knew she wasn't supposed to drink out of someone else's drink.

Jeremy came and set the drinks down. "My mother always told me not to take a drink if I didn't actually get it."

"Seems like good advice. Hey wait. These are good. Seriously, I'm not going to put drugs in your drink."

"I know you wouldn't. But Jeremy I just took a big swig from that table thinking it was ours."

"You don't say?"

That's when they saw the scuffle and the big security guy came and told the dude to leave. Kristan wondered what that was all about but she didn't have to wait long as an emergency vehicle pulled up and some girl was taken away by ambulance. She was breathing and somewhat awake but looked like she hit her head. Or maybe someone hit her. Then Kristan felt a little dizzy and asked Noah to take her back to her dorm room. The night was over. He obliged and made sure she didn't need some other help. Did she think she drank something weird?

"No. I don't think so I just feel groggy."

Once she got into Jeremy's car she fell fast asleep.

She knew she was being driven but it felt like a dream. Very dreamy. She saw the large white mansion with beautiful gardens. They were headed in the right direction. Jeremy played some music at a low volume which was soothing. She remembered they had had the perfect date even if they weren't partners, sexual, dating, or otherwise. She thought in life everyone needs a nice friend and she had just made one. Perfect friends. Just is.

Maybe that was a poem title, "Just Is." When she would awaken the next day that would be the very last thing she would remember. She just couldn't wake up. She could only dream and so she did. One after the other and they were all from her senior year in high school. Maybe this is what happened to that girl she worked with. She called her one night trying to remember the events which occurred when they went out with two new boys they'd met. Kristan drifted away as Jeremy drove back to campus. Every now and then he would shake her arm and she responded, so all was good he thought. Maybe he should stay with her all night. That way he would know for sure. He was certain she didn't take anything herself knowingly. He smiled. She would be all right he just knew but to be safe he would stay and sleep on the floor on her big rug.

Once he had her up to her dorm room he helped her up to bed and told her he was staying. She said, "Okay."

The first two hours he wakened her and asked if she was okay and she replied, "I'm fine."

Kristan on the other hand was reliving a friend's nightmare. Now she understood. When she called her the next day telling her the story she was so thankful her friend was still alive. Graduation parties were being held and students were visiting others homes and parties. Her friend would never know for sure but she was left in the middle of an intersection with the car running. Someone had drugged her and left her there as cars swirled by until someone called the police. Her graduation cards and money was gone too. They drugged her, then robbed her, now she was in court suffering the consequences of bad choices. The bad choice was trusting people who couldn't be trusted. Kristan let out a big sigh and tears ran down her cheek. Jeremy got up and saw this. She said she was okay just remembering a very sad spring day. Later Kristan found out these two guys were robbing houses and dealing drugs. She knew what her mother would say, "These two guys are preying upon y'all. You must be careful, especially as they are older. Oh honey, I wish I could teach you everything all at once."

The words *everyone is not nice Kristan. Bad people exist.* These phrases would leave her mother's mouth the very day in the garden outside the dorms when she left just as she had spoken about the incident last spring. It only angered her mother more when she told her she was with one of them. Just is.

In the morning Kristan woke up, feeling groggy, but definitely okay. Jeremy was asleep on her big rug. He had stayed the night. What a great friend! She went to her fridge and retrieved a bottle of water and drank it down. Come to think of it she was hungry.

"Hey, you hungry? She asked.

"Very!" he replied.

"Let's go load up our plates. And then head to Fort Knox. I feel ready."

"Wonder what he'll wear today? Maybe he'll be in swim shorts and sandals."

"Like a summer day …" they said in unison.

It was a perfect summer day as the pair walked briskly to breakfast. College was fun.

Chapter 5). Goodbye from the Camelia Garden

Later that day Kristan took a long nap and reflected back on that very day her mother and father dropped her off and left her there at college.

The drive was long to Vista College in South Georgia, over four hours from North Atlanta via I-75. They decided to go the night before and stay in a hotel room, therefore they could arrive on time and not be tired out. Likely many had the same idea for when they arrived the car line was long, and the luggage and belongings that needed to go up to the dorms added to the outdoor heat from the August sun. Her mother's beauty had long ago faded into a middle aged attractive woman who worked out, read, ate well and loved her new husband. She was devoted. How she got so lucky twice in one life was beyond her view. Maybe because her new husband was very attentive. He knew he had a good thing and loved her, adored her and doted on her. They especially liked to travel, eat out and read books. He even played the piano for her at times. He was slender, ate small meals and smoked a few cigars now and then. He liked bourbon and card playing as well. They fit well together. Life was pleasurable.

Helpers were everywhere but elevators were in demand and short supply. Kristans mother was not about to walk up six flights of stairs with luggage in hand. She would wait in the lobby. The whole process seemed like going to a birthday-slumber party that you didn't know the parents and had you wondering if you were doing the right thing leaving your precious cargo all night long, and didn't feel right until the next day when you picked your child up and they were still alive. That and now the child was 18 not nine. Were you doing the right thing? One wondered and the more the afternoon time progressed the worse Kristan's mother felt. How can one let the ties that bind go? How can one soften the blow upon departure? Solace in knowing there will be another time? In the future? But when? Think about all the times service men or women left their spouses and children behind. What of the one who waits, worries, and wonders while the one going is busy, traveling and has others nearby as close comrades? Surely saying goodbye won't be too bad. Will it? We'll see her in a month or two they say to one another. And she is making friends and going to get an education. Isn't that special and living the American dream? Why does it cost so much? She'd be better off going to a community college and not spending thousands of dollars to party with strangers. Yes. But then it wouldn't be college nor growing up learning to defend ones principles. She doesn't even know her principles as yet. Must they be tested so early in life?

Kristan's mother Chloe would not even experience the worst of the coming goodbye until it hit her like a ton of bricks when after she was strapped in the car seat and the car pulled away, and she could no longer see her child, her only child. The sobs came with breathing sighs and tears trickling down the cheeks but as each block was driven out of town the intensity came stronger and stronger. By the time the car was back on the highway she let it out and sobbed such loud sighs of anguish, one might think she'd just lost a child or husband, possibly even a parent. She had only dropped them off to attend college. The bond was breaking on the highway and her husband never said a word. After thirty minutes Chloe began to calm down. It surprised her that she cried with such intensity. Her whole body seemed to be involved. When they had walked out into the garden where she saw the plaque, recognizing the women before her who had done good deeds, it became apparent to Chloe, moms receive so much love it's difficult to give it up. One who gives love and receives it back is a nice thing. She took a picture of the garden plaque and decided she might paint it or write a poem giving credit to the moms who help their kids go on. The days and pain would wain and she relished that she had loved so much. Nothing could be greater she thought in her mind. This made her smile.

A week later, however briefly traumatized she had been, now it was gone. Until ... one morning she clutched her chest on the left side and upon scratching she realized she had a case of the shingles. Shingles are painful and virus like. You cannot make them go away. For Chloe she blamed it on the pain endured by a departure for which she had no concept how she would feel. Wow. She had not heard before how horrible it is to leave your kids at college. Maybe she was different maybe she was crazy but for her it was crushingly horrible the day of departure. Maybe she was traumatized after all by her husband's death in the car all those years ago. Maybe some people can't wait to drop their kids off wanting them to be out of their hair and be gone to not bother them anymore. Anymore. That was it. The finality.

One day here one day gone. Well, now it's over she decided, except she had shingles on her left chest from front to back. She was heartsick; my love is gone. But not forever even though it seems that way. What now? Chloe was not sure but the shingles took two and half weeks to depart, much longer than it took to say goodbye. She thought it dire that they surrounded her heart. Nasty shingles.

Chloe painted the Camelia Garden and the plaque from the garden next to the Vista University. She would give this as a present to her family at Christmas time. She also wrote a few poems and thought about one of her favorite poets, Poe.

Poe

What is the Poe in poetry?

I'd likely say yes, there is.

A female unmarried is just a Ms.

But a divorced or widowed woman

Slices her heart then

Paints poetry on a canvas

Or lays it in a brain canal.

Why is there Poe in poetry?

Poe in poetry it is.

His madness fed the lines

Over and over.

Rap, Tap, Tap

Make a sound

Drink a round.

I saw the light

On the brain scan

And knew twenty years ago

The notes that made me feel.

Let's listen to one another

And feel with our nerves.

Rap, Tap, Tap.

And so it continued a special relationship over the miles on a new playing field. But it would be tumultuous and sparring, and reveling in unknowns for quite some time. Such is life. It never ends. The first time Chloe and Kristan did a face time seemed surreal. She'd seen and watched her over and over do this with her friends but Kristan always came home so there was no need. Facetime. Wow. So cool. We sure didn't have this back in the nineties thought her mom. While the world was busy developing the phones and technology, and forever altering the world- the world was adapting and changing because of it. Would this be good or would evil set in before we knew it and get a hold of our lives? For now all was good. The shingles left, her sister told her she could have had a vaccine. She'd never heard of a vaccine for shingles. Too late now she'd had them and likely the antibodies were now circulating for future psychological trauma. The long lasting bodily pain from shingles far outset the sad time saying goodbye. Chloe would tell a few of her friends to ready themselves.

Whomever said wisdom comes with the ages was certainly correct. You learn the hard way. Listen up to those grandparents who are never around anymore because they live seven states over. No wonder kids are messed up they don't have their elders!

Chloe went out to lunch with her friend and listened to this and that. Nothing really seemed important anymore especially other people's kids. But when her girlfriend started talking about a new boyfriend, she asked to see a picture. She couldn't believe it. It was the same two guys that had parlayed or preyed upon her own daughter and friend. What was happening? The shock on her face must have said more than she was willing to give because now her friend wanted to know everything. She should tell her and warn her. Maybe nothing would happen, maybe it would. She decided to tell the information because if she didn't and something happened-things could be worse off. If my best friend didn't warn me then who would? Mothers are very protective of their daughters. The old cliché is a dad with a shotgun but let me tell you a mother will stand in front of a freight train for her child. That is a mother's love. Remember the momma bear and her cubs. Don't mess with this. That much is true. After she had lunch with her and a few days passed, someone wasn't going out with so and so anymore. It was settled. Danger had come in and a good person warned another. That is the right thing to do.

Chloe thought back to all the times at the bus stop, school functions in elementary school, and even church choir. There were many a good times with her friends and their children. They'd grown up together. This would be felt for a lifetime. She smiled. Now it was over. What's next? Something, but it might not be as good as we had. Life. It's like that. Over before you took it all in. Or maybe you waited and now it's so good. Does it have to be over? Or you had the best. Now what? Memories. Chloe smiled again. She wanted to live before she had to give again. It was her turn. Yup. It's my turn was her brand new slogan. Imagine that.

Kristan and Chloe did a Facetime on a Friday night a few weeks after Kristan got to school. It was neat as her mother might say. Not planned just spontaneous and joyful. Chloe poured herself a wine and daughter did likewise but didn't show her mom. One could still hide some things from momma when they needed to even during a Facetime call. Chloe showed her the pets wondering about her home.

"Speak loud so she can hear you," as her mother put the camera on the family cat named Lilly.

"Meow, meow."

"Fill me in on the homecoming or parent's weekend coming up."

"Sure. You and dad will come on a Friday and we'll go to the football game, there'll be food, drinks, and music beforehand. Then we'll watch the game, go home and catch up the next morning. Dinner will be anything we want on Saturday night and then a quick brunch Sunday morning. You don't have to do anything really, only if you want to." Kristan gave her the update.

"Sounds like just a weekend for all the parents to hang around, so all the students are in the same boat at once."

"You aced it mom. You can meet a couple friends I've made at the football game."

"Sounds good. What else is up?" Mom asked.

"Noah has asked me to go to the beach with him the following weekend near the beginning of November. His grandmother's condo is empty. I said yes." Kristan waited for her mother's reply. She didn't care just waited for a response. Things were quiet over the phone.

Chloe wasn't sure what to say. What should she say? She hesitated. No words. Silence.

"Mom. I'm breaking up with him. It's a breakup weekend."

"Like saying goodbye. That can be hard."

"I'm going to keep it positive like you always do. I get a fantastic weekend on the beach and the rest of my life is free for endless possibilities."

"Kristan?"

"Yes, mom." She could hear her mother's silent tone. She was about to say something very serious.

"I'm not sure if I should bring this up but remember the girl named Rebekka who died at the quarry near the river?"

"Vaguely, I know you said they live near us."

"Yes, she did."

"I think she was much older, that's why I didn't know her. We weren't in school at the same time." Kristan explained.

"It came down to cybercrimes via the internet and phone surveillance. The local police were involved with surveillance and wiretapping. That poor girl Maria and her daughter Hope got mixed up in it due to a distant relative. It's a total mess with the courts involved."

"What do you mean courts? Like lawyers and judges and agencies?" Kristan questioned.

"Exactly. She was targeted to get to her aunt who was defending her grandson quietly."

"So is it about money?" Kristan asked.

"I think the paper said it's about control of people, businesses, and cases involved in the courts."

"Another words it's huge. Should I be worried?"

"I don't think so. Keep your Social Medias to private and watch who you follow. I think that's the best advice I can give."

"I know that that Maria girl ended up in a private hospital. Someone who babysits for her and others told me."

"Yes, I heard that too. Because she was almost killed by a sword before the cops came and saved her. I just want you to remember there are bad people out there looking to scam others, steal from others, even rape or kill others. I don't understand it all but it happens. Promise me you'll be safe. Safe as you can be."

"Mom, I will. And I will watch out on the internet. I know they can turn your phone and camera on remotely. I saw that in a movie."

"That does not make me feel better!"

"I'm sorry."

"Stay in groups. Remember what I always told you, never leave anyone alone at night anywhere."

"That rule I will always remember. Thanks mom."

Chapter 6). Sororities & Fraternities

Kristan wasn't sure which sorority she liked best. She had a few picked out. Who would pick her? It didn't really matter, she wasn't too fussy; her mother had never joined one and survived just fine. She was doing it for the future parties, and of course, friendship. It's just that here at Vista the boys had a Frat house for freshman but the girls did not. Oh well, she liked her dorm as it was close to everything but not the interior. She had started working out swimming laps at the pool and was feeling energized and happy. One of the other pledges told her she got wind of a party this very coming weekend. She said all the new pledges were invited. Sweet. It was a Frat party that started at noon on Saturday. Fun. Yeah. Right. If her mother only knew she was going to be partying at noon on Saturday-she'd likely come pick her up and make her stay at home. Best not tell mom Kristan thought. She didn't. Be selective on disclosure. She was learning how to be a young adult at eighteen.

At the end of day three for pledging they took pictures with the other pledges near the fountain which was the center of campus. She sent a couple of these home to mom via her phone. Mom was pleased. It looked like college was going smoothly.

"Two more days and we find out which sorority we made," Taylor said excitedly.

"Then we'll be on our way into Greek life," replied Kristan not really understanding all of it. She pretended to grasp the idea. For her it was just a set a friends, girls and guys, with who she would be hanging out with from time to time.

"Hey we should go to the Bean Dip Friday after we find out to celebrate." Kristan had made friends with Taylor and it occurred to her they might not be in the same group.

"Let's do that. We can meet there and bring a few others. Sound good?"

"Perfect. See you Friday for the announcement and then dinner."

Later back at her dorm Kristan was pleased her and Taylor had made a date for Friday night. What if it was she herself that didn't get chosen? What a thought! It was possible. She had heard about someone trying and not being selected. Good grief wasn't there a place for everyone? Maybe she shouldn't have tried to get into an exclusive club which excludes others. Oh brother. She did not like worrying about this load. What garbage. She had better things to do like study for her other four classes. She did like English the best. It must be the teacher that makes it fun and curious to know more.

In the depths of studying and oblivious to the outside world Kristan was getting ahead and extremely prepared for her classes. She wouldn't have to open a book this weekend, except maybe Sunday if she wanted to for pleasure. She looked over at her window and saw a flashing blue and red light. What was that? It seemed to be right outside her window towards the Frat houses across the street. What's going on on a Wednesday night? She got up and looked out after turning her light off. She could see an ambulance waiting outside one of the houses across the street. A couple police cars were parked there as well. Then there was a knock at her door.

"Kristan, Kristan you in there?" She recognized the voice of her hall monitor.

"Yes, I'm here."

"I'm just taking a head count with the activity going on across the street."

"Yeah. I hope they are okay."

"I don't think they are. An ambulance and two cop cars doesn't look good."

"What do you think it might be?" Kristan wanted to get her opinion.

"Overdose. It's always an overdose. Single story house so no falls. Could be a fight but I doubt it, it's not the weekend. Those usually happen on the weekend."

"Good to know."

Kristan watched as they brought out a stretcher with someone on it. Quickly they loaded it up onto the ambulance and away they sped off to the hospital she surmised. Just the other night she had heard about a student death by gunshot when he went to buy some drugs on the edge of town. How come she never heard about all this tragedy before at home? Probably because she didn't watch the news, only her mother took all that terrible news in so she could alert her daughter what to do, not do, and who to stay away from. The Frat party was

Saturday and she hoped they didn't cancel it but they might. Friday at 2:00 was the announcement. She closed her books and went to bed. Should she alert her mother about the ambulance? No sense as it was already late and what could she do but worry?

On Friday Taylor and Kristan walked to the hall where the announcement was going to be posted. After that there would be a small get together for an hour then nothing would begin for a week. It all seemed so drawn out thought Kristan. Once the posting was up they walked quickly over to find out their destiny. Kristan saw her name with one of the three that she liked. Good. It was over. No more worries. She helped Taylor find her name and it was not there. Kristan helped her some more looking over all the sororities.

"Are they all posted?" asked Kristan to Taylor.

"I believe so." Taylor hit herself on the thigh. Why did she even try? Seriously, this is for the birds. Crap. She thought. What now? She guessed she would have to get a job or a boyfriend instead of a sorority.

"It's even better. You can be my guest when I go to parties. You don't have to pay the dues and you just come with me. No one will know. It's perfect. All the benefits without the hassle. Man I should have done it that way," Kristan babbled on for her friend's dear sake. What on earth could she do-she had to help her new friend?

Taylor looked at Kristan. She really meant it. She had a point. Benefits. "No dues, only the fun. Why not?"

The two of them hugged and left the postings. Today Kristan would not go to the hour long hello party. She would cheer up her friend and then go to The Bean Dip.

At four thirty Kristan and Taylor went to The Bean Dip and sat at a table. Levi joined them as he had done the lunch shift and was off for the weekend.

"Did y'all hear about the guy that almost died last night?" Levi said.

"No but I saw an ambulance across the street near the frat houses."

"Do you know what happened?" asked Taylor. Though she didn't really care about anything at this moment she wanted to be friendly to Levi. She thought he was cute and very nice.

"I do. The dude works here so I got the full story. They were mixing big time last night and using the beer bong to deliver some toxic doses."

"Toxic? You mean liquor?"

"Yes. Just liquor but it goes in fast. The dude went crazy and then unconscious."

They are warning the campus, especially the Greek houses, they will close down the parties. There has to be a cop at every party now going forward. He's there to monitor not close it down."

"Sounds like that's a good idea. But he'll just be watching a bunch of drunk college kids." Kristan didn't know how this would help.

"Watching. But making sure no one dies, apparently." Levi added.

Kristan and Taylor paused with this knowledge letting it sink in. Guys are the ones that usually got out of control. The girls thought this made the party a little safer for all. Kristan and Taylor ordered food. They were starved! Levi didn't ask the girls about getting into the sorority. He figured they would tell him. So it must have not gone well. He might ask Taylor later tonight back at her dorm as they had a tentative date to watch a show together at ten.

"Hey guys I left something out in my car. I'll be right back," said Kristan. She walked out and there was a white van next to her navy blue car. A creepy guy smoking a cigarette was standing at the rear of his van. Was it a work van? Seemed to be. She noticed the tags or plates said South Carolina. Must be work. She got into her car and called her mother feeling rather weird from the stalker next to her. She remembered to lock the car when getting in but not before she looked out to see the guy. His hands were on the back seat handle, or so she thought. "Jesus, Mary and Joseph," she whispered.

"Kristan?" Her mother answered.

"Oh mom, the creepiest thing just happened."

"What? Are you okay? Where are you? It's broad daylight so it can't be too bad."

"I know. I'm fine. Just a guy standing next to a van from South Carolina looking stalkerish." Kristan relayed.

"Stalkerish. What's stalkerish? Either they are or they aren't."

"Yes. Stalkerish. Definitely."

"Do you need to call 911?"

"My friends are in the restaurant. I'm good. I don't see him anymore."

"Where are you at so I know?"

"The Bean Dip. You know I think I'm on edge because there was a party last night and someone almost died."

"Died? How do you know? Oh honey. College is frightening."

"I know. Right?"

The van pulled away. Kristan settled down. Her mother kept talking. She told her she made a sorority but her friend did not. Everything calmed down and Kristan went back in to join her friends.

Kristan went back to her dorm and Levi and Taylor made their way to Taylor's place. They watched a show together and ended the night with a light slow kiss. Taylor was almost asleep at midnight when her friend next door knocked and woke her. They were going dancing down the highway. Did she want to come? They said it would be fun. For some reason she said yes. Maybe it was the rejection from earlier today, maybe she needed to find a new way or what she was cut out for. She went. She didn't make it home until 5:00 in the morning. Energized from dancing but not wanting anyone to see her she slid into her room and fell fast asleep but not before wondering what just happened.

At 10:00 the knock at the door was persistent. Oh yeah. Levi was coming to take her for coffee and breakfast. And at 12:00 Kristan was picking her up and they were walking to a Frat party, an all-day Frat party. Bathing suits required. Slip and slide fun. Protected by a police officer. Saturday. Just another typical day at college. Let's go.

"Taylor, I forgot to ask you about the sorority posting?" he asked.

"You did?"

"Should I not? Tell me. I'm sorry. I should have kept quiet."

"No. No. It's okay. I had a chance to sleep on it. I feel better today."

"So you didn't find one that suited you?"

"On the other hand they didn't choose me. Hey, what's not to like?"

"My thoughts. Did you check all the boards? Maybe you just didn't get in the one you wanted but another chose you." He kept talking and talking.

She stared at him intently. She cocked her head to the side. "I never thought of that. Kristan did get one of the three she chose. I checked mine and not one of them listed my name."

"Well. We know where to go then. To the boards!"

Chapter 7. Saturday Fraternity Party

Taylor, bikini clad with cover up on raced, Levi, to the sorority board listing. She didn't want to raise her depleted hopes but maybe he was right. Levi, on the other hand was sure she got in. The excitement to get coffee on a Saturday was raised way beyond any normal goals in life. This had to be. Her. Day.

Kristan had gone home early and had the most restful night since landing here at Vista University. Nothing was bothering her. Even the shitty looking guy from the van standing next to her car that had creeped her out was released from her vision once she told her mother about it. Dude was probably looking for some helpless victim and that was not going to be her. However, the thought crossed her mind some girls are not prepared, not looking for danger. Of course, her mother had to inform her about all the bad dudes in the world and how they can look like nice guys. Oh mom, thanks for that. Was Levi good or bad? Was Jeremy good or bad? She decided if they were in college she would give them the benefit of the doubt. In other words those guys would have to prove themselves irregular or bad. One or two wrong things she'd cancel them off her list. That's how she would protect herself. At least she didn't live in the dark ages where there was no choice, no freedoms or thoughts allowed.

Kristan had coffee in her room this morning, half of an iced latte from yesterday with a packet of her favorite oatmeal. She opened her closet and went to the swimsuits to find the perfect one for today. She wanted to stand out, get noticed or whatever. She wanted to feel pretty. She chose the red bikini with a bow on the back bottoms. Her buttocks were exposed. All was cool with her age group- she saw many of these on the beach. Her mother had never seen her in anything like this. Ever. Oh well, moms not here. Yippee. She put it on and snapped a few Instagram photos, along with a quick snapchat. Kristan was ready for a fun day!

She left her room at 11:30, to pick up Taylor, then they would both walk to the fraternity houses which were all on one street.

On the way to Taylor's room Kristan looked down to the end of the hallway where a rec room held, Taylor and Levi, embraced in a passionate kiss. Kristan walked slower until she finally met up with them. Taylor was brimming with joy.

"Hey guys, all right. Y'all have been busy hanging out." Kristan flounced around.

They smiled at her and one another.

"Okay. Come on. What's up?" Kristan asked.

"What's up?" Taylor toyed with her for a short while.

"I give. Y'all in love?"

They laughed. "Kristan, I got in!!!"

"Got in?"

"A sorority."

"You did. That's fantastic!"

"It is. Now I can hang out with you and we can do sorority things like frat parties and cleanup on Sundays." Taylor rattled on.

"That's right tomorrow is cleanup the park day."

"I'll come help if that's okay. Tomorrow, what time?" Levi asked.

"Yes. They said bring friends if you wanted to. Begins at nine."

"Girls, I've got to run. This is Saturday which means study day for me. I study all day every Saturday and then work tonight until midnight. But I can join you at nine in the morning."

"See you tomorrow at nine at the turn around. They are driving us by bus to the park," Kristan added.

"Thanks for the coffee. And for thinking I got in when I didn't."

Taylor was having a great day and it showed. They waved goodbye then headed for the elevators to make their way over to frat row. They had no idea of what they were in for. What could happen during a day party from 12-6 at a fraternity house with a policeman standing guard? Nothing, right?

The girls arrived and made the rounds of introducing themselves, snacking, trying the punch, and watching the slip n slide out front and some of the other games. The girls eventually found a cooler with White Claw cans and opened one for each. This would be a safer bet than drinking out of a punch bowl with God knows what in it. Some of the dudes were playing beer pong and other games. Taylor and Kristan watched, laughed some and found themselves trying the slip and slide. The cool water felt good and refreshing. By three o'clock each of them felt buzzed and were definitely having a good time. They had met loads of dudes and a few other girls from different sororities.

The pizza arrived. "Thank you!" said one of the guys. "Pizza. Spread the word."

Taylor and Kristan made a plate and went out front where the party held even more students. Kristan saw the cop. He was standing over next to a police car parked in the driveway of the house next door. Watching the partygoers. Was he there to stop a fight? Yes. That had to be it. Kristan would later learn as a sophomore that upperclassmen had to have a security guard and/or policeman to watch a party. That was standard protocol for fraternities and sororities as of a few years ago when hazing had become a dangerous sport for the Greek community. There was comfort in the knowing someone could be spot on making sense of the lined garbage can party. She smiled.

"My mom has come a few weekends early because she can't make it on Parents Weekend. She can pick us up, take us back and drop us off while she gets ready for dinner. We want a ride, right?"

"Yes. I'm with you. It is a far walk-even though I need it."

"She'll be here in 10 minutes. That's five o'clock."

"Perfect."

Taylor's mother drove down the row of houses and saw a police car in a driveway but she wasn't to the house yet. She kept going around the curve and made her way back to a cul-de-sac where she saw another police car. This time the cop was standing outside his car. She saw bikini clad buttocks exposed on a long blond haired girl talking with her daughter. Her daughter looked at her and pointed. The red bikini girl was her friend and the two of them started walking to her car. They had red solo cups. They got in the car and offered her a drink. She took the cup, smelled it, and then poured it out the window.

"There will be no drinking in my car ladies."

"Mom, it's a party."

"What is that policeman doing at the party?"

"He's the guard."

"Oh my. Protection. Okay. That's good. Y'all know you can't drink in a car, right?"

"Right. But you are driving." Taylor spoke up. The two of them surely didn't need their buzz broken yet.

"Yes. I know. Thankfully." Taylor's mother said.

"Mrs. Smith, we take Uber to get around, especially for parties. But thanks today for picking us up."

"You're welcome. Ladies, please be safe. And congratulations on getting in your sororities."

Kristan and Taylor clanked their solo cups together and took a swig while her mother shook her head back and forth. The girls had brought her a solo cup of punch but she politely declined spilling the liquid outside before she took off driving. A cop she thought. At first her mind raced to the idea that there was trouble and maybe someone was getting arrested. That was one way of making sure the youth didn't misspend an ordinary Saturday Fraternity party.

Taylor's new friend Levi was working tonight so she and her mom went out to eat. But first they visited a museum on the way before the reservation. Her mother had been into gardening rather zealously and she wanted to visit the historic women's museum nearby. It was in an old plantation style home with pillars, Georgian architecture, she supposed. Her mother had to work her whole life as a single parent so she never involved herself in clubs up until now. If that's what her mother wanted to do, so be it. Her mother told her she bought two acres, almost farm like in size and planned on having multiple gardens. Go for it mom, I'll come visit she thought. Mrs. Smith was glad Taylor seemed to be settling in very nice at college. If only it wasn't so expensive with dorms, apartments, food, and tuition. Taylor needed to study to obtain the HOPE Scholarship, then both of their lives would be easier.

"Taylor, we are going to the Crescent, it is part of the Garden Center, Inc. They have gardens and a few buildings. Apparently, the very first garden club in America was in Athens, Georgia. Can you believe it? Well, everything has to start somewhere. I just want to find out about their resources and how and when to plant my garden. It will be nice to see something already in place."

"Sure mother. Whatever you say."

"You might even like it. It is a place where they have weddings and other parties."

"I will get you flowers for Christmas. Do they sell any?"

"I am not sure. But we'll find out."

They never did find any plants for sale but Taylor saw a beautiful Christmas ornament she knew her mother would love, and if you bought five then it was only twenty dollars. It was the gorgeous crescent home with pillars and a garden surrounding the circular front porch with magenta camellias, or so she thought. Lovely. She'd give one to Kristan and her mother, in addition to her own mother, and maybe, Levi. She'd save one for herself. How about that her Christmas shopping was finished and she just started? Suddenly, she remembered the poem read in class by Kristans mother. Wasn't it Magenta Blood? Eerie. She shook the goosebumps off her skin and carried on with the purchase. Spirituality about life and death, being in between, neither alive nor dead, that was what was going on. Her poem was very spiritual.

The next morning all three gathered at the turnaround with a fresh coffee from inside the student center. Clean up would be fun because they were all doing it together. They could talk, pick up trash, sweep sidewalks, put down pine straw around bushes and trees, cut dead limbs, prune a few trees so the walkways laid an easier path. They even painted a picnic bench. This was nice doing something for others future enjoyment as a volunteer.

"How was the visit with your mother?" Kristan asked.

"We had a good time, went to a museum and then dinner downtown."

"I went home and slept and slept, all night long."

"Girls, I went to work and we had the busiest Saturday of the whole year."

"I'm so sorry. You okay?"

"Sure, free food fixes many things."

"Ha ha. I bet." Taylor said. She understood the money thing. She'd had a job all through high school and her mother made her save 50% of it. That ended up being a good thing. She had thousands of dollars and didn't need to work the first year or two. Her mother told her to study hard, get the HOPE scholarship and your college will be almost paid for. Levi was an athlete but didn't get a scholarship-yet, he was so close. He planned on working during college all four or five years. He wanted to be a Jacques Cousteau and study the sea. This school had the program so here he was. He was a swimmer but didn't get any money for college. Money went to the big games like football and basketball, definitely not swimming. His mother had little money and no husband, therefore, he had no father. His new girlfriend, Taylor, wants to study law and plans on making many changes for the better. He had no idea how she was going to do that. Maybe she didn't even know. But she wanted to try and change the world. He didn't know how Kristan was going to pay for college but she didn't look worried. Maybe student loans or the HOPE scholarship. She wasn't working as yet. She did have a mother and a father who both worked. Likely she was set. He did hear her say she use to swim.

"Kristan, did you swim in high school?"

"Yes, I did, all the time. I swam year round. You?"

"I did too. We'll have to meet at the pool sometime."

"Sure I'd love that."

"Can I come and watch?" Taylor asked.

Chapter 8. Noah Comes

"You always say that momma," retorted Noah. "What does it mean?"

"What does what mean?"

"Cool beans!" he shouted.

"Noah," she paused. "I don't know. Let me google it."

"Oh brother," he replied.

"What does oh brother mean?" His mom asked politely. One more year, in fact this time next year he'll be in the air force, or navy. She crossed her fingers. For sure he'll get in. She looked up to heaven and said a little prayer. *Please God* she begged. She asked her dead husband for help too.

"It means I'm leaving. Love you momma. And thank Grandma Mary for the condo in St. Simons. I'll love her forever."

"Noah, you're welcome. Clean up before you leave."

"Will do."

"Noah, cool beans means wonderful or excited. I'm excited for you to see your girlfriend."

"Me too. Bye."

"Bye now. See you Monday."

Noah had quite a drive ahead of him. Atlanta to Vista University was about four hours, he'd pick her up, and then both of them would travel over to St. Simons Island. They'd find his grandma's condo named Oceanside and stay for the weekend. He figured they would arrive between four and five o'clock, check in, go for dinner, come back and maybe walk the beach a little before going to bed. He was excited for that part too. They had been dating ten months already and both of them had talked about doing it. Now seemed like the perfect time.

Kristan had slept in, then packed for the weekend. It was a long weekend for high school and college classes with Friday and Monday off. Noah was coming today to pick her up. They'd arrive tonight at the condo have dinner and walk the beach. Saturday and Sunday could be spent at the pool or beach with walks and bike rides, maybe shopping then cooking together. She felt so grown up. These are the things one gets to do when becoming an adult. Was eighteen an adult or was it twenty one? That's when it hit her this is the practice time from eighteen until you hit twenty one when it was all on you. Everything. *Good, I've got a few years to work on it* she thought.

She packed two bikinis and one tank suit, shorts, tops, and a sundress along with her shampoo, dryer, towel, and some sandals. She packed a few jewelry items and very little makeup. She wanted to look good but what did it matter she was breaking up with him. Wait. What was she thinking? How can I break up at the end of the weekend? Maybe I should tell him the first day-then, I'll have it over with. No. No. Oh dear. The more she thought about it the shakier she got. She was actually worried. She didn't want to hurt his feelings. But what about her? She was important too. In the end she made the plan that it would be Sunday over coffee as they tasted some delicious breakfast. That way nothing would be spoiled for the first two days, and later, on Sunday they could walk the beach as friends. By the time Monday came the drive home would be peaceful, friendly and they would depart with a goodbye hug. They needed to be full in on where they were in their lives. He a senior and she a freshman. All packed she charged her phone and grabbed some lunch at the cafeteria. She returned and took a nap before Noah came.

A knock on the door wakened her. She looked at her phone and it was too early for Noah.

"Yes. Who is it?"

"Kristan, it's Jeremy," he replied.

"Okay. Hi. Come in."

"I know you are getting ready to go away for the weekend. Sarah told me."

"I do want you to have a good time. Seriously, I do. Maybe it's the poetry and sonnets we're studying but I feel like we are just getting going in college and I don't want you to be held back."

"You mean by a guy?"

"Yeah. I'm sorry. I'm intruding."

"No. You are not intruding. You are being a friend. And that's what we decided. So it's okay you tell me what a friend might say."

"Remember, I picked the romance play and sonnet. You picked the summer day," he explained.

"I also picked the summer night play," she added and turned to look away.

He touched her on the shoulder. "Be safe. And I'm here for you this freshman year!"

"Thank you. I'm going to have fun, be safe, and say goodbye to high school. I'm going to set us both free."

"I like the way you put that. See you Tuesday in class."

"Tuesday. Goodbye."

"Bye."

She had to admit that was nice to have someone care about you that wasn't your mother. She smiled. Then the door opened and it was Noah. It had not been closed all the way. They likely passed each other in the elevator or hallway.

"Noah. I'm so excited. Are you?"

"Are you kidding? Let's go."

The pair swept up her belongings and made haste for his car. Kristan bought a couple of cokes for the trip from the vending and off they were. Music playing, Noah driving, and the road ahead to take them away. Kristan snapped a few photos and put them to Instagram. She took one of Noah but placed that on her private Instagram. She had a feeling she would maintain this certain high feeling all weekend. That very thought made her smile. Oh yeah!

Kristan closed her eyes and thought about her Shakespeare picks. Could it be she instinctively picked a summer night and a summer day? Did she secretly want this to occur?

Absolutely. It must be. It's in the cards as her mom would say. She wanted to feel the pleasure of love. Because she had fallen in love with Noah, maybe it was puppy love, but it felt real. And she would like to experience the joy of that mother earth feeling. It wasn't lewd or nasty but right. After all she was away from her mother now and out from prying eyes or questions. She didn't have to sneak and this was a preview of things to come. One did a little practice to get better at something. Swimming taught her that. God was allowing this to happen. He was okay with this. To be or not to be, that is the question. And she will be having sex, this weekend.

On the way into St. Simons Noah stopped at a grocery store to buy goods. "How about we cook on Sunday and eat out tonight and Saturday? Sound good?"

"Perfecto. Want me to buy some wine with my fake ID?"

"You have one of those?"

"Yes, all the girls got one. Most of the time it works."

"Maybe a six pack of beer and a bottle or two of wine."

"It works best if I go through the check out and you bring the car up."

"Ok miss. You're in charge," he handed her that one.

He was right there and helped her with the groceries. The whole plan was set. Now they just needed to relax, go for a walk on the beach and get some dinner. And, of course, check in.

"The King and Prince, sounds like a fancy place," she read the sign and saw a yellow colored hotel on the beach. They kept driving and eventually came to the beautifully landscaped condos nestled right before the dunes which touched the beach.

"Gorgeous. Look there's the ocean. It's so beautiful. Can we go for a walk right after we settle in?" She asked.

"Yes. Sure."

They were on the second floor which gave them a spectacular view of the ocean and horizon. The condo was large with three bedrooms and lovely glass doors leading to a patio. Kristan put away the groceries and Noah poured them each a beer in a plastic cup to go for a walk.

"Let me unpack my things first and I'll be right there." The place was fantastic. Noah found the radio and turned on some music. Kristan turned a few lights on for when they came back. In a couple hours it would be dark and she would only hear the roar of the ocean and maybe notes of soft jazz music. All her romance novels had one thing in common when the bedroom scene occurred: soft background music, jazzy like vocals, and memorable words spoken by say Nora Jones or the fabulous Sade.

She hoped Noah was prepared in the guy type of way. Certainly his friend, or even his mother, had told him to come prepared. Of course, forget about it. All guys were ready, especially after dating this long.

The young couple, hand in hand, walked the quiet beach. The waves barely lapped the sand. The sun had set behind the trees and there was no moon. In the distance they heard a motorboat but saw no boat. It was a dead night for sure. Noah stopped, leaned over and kissed Kristan.

Just a kiss.

"Ready?"

"I am." She replied.

It was like a bad play. The winning team had fumbled the ball and the only hope left was praying the other team didn't run and score with no time left.

The music wouldn't turn on. In fact the electricity seemed to be out. Noah found a candle and lit it. Kristan changed into her camisole slip, and together they found the bed. Kissing, and touching, then exploring, all quieting newcomer nerves. When the time came it came fast and Noah looked right at Kristan and smiled. Kristan held Noah's cheeks and this was it. Over so quickly she thought. First time jitters.

"Oh, no!" he quietly exclaimed.

"Noah?"

"I forgot the condom," he explained.

"You what?"

"Yup, I forgot to put it on."

"I thought to ask but I thought that's what you did in the bathroom."

"No, I fixed my hair."

"Oh, no." Kristan thought about what she should do. She didn't have a plan.

"I'm so sorry but I think I know what to do," he said.

"We never ate dinner-so, I'll order a pizza and we'll go to the pool. We'll go swimming."

"Yeah, then the chlorine will get rid of the sperm."

"Except, it's probably a salt water pool. They all are nowadays."

"I think swimming is the cure. I'm going right now. You order the pizza. Have them bring it to the pool."

"Good idea." He kissed her. He fucked up. He really fucked up.

After swimming and eating pizza, they drank a beer from their red cups. It would be okay. Nobody ever gets pregnant the first time. No way. Never.

When they finally went to bed that very first night Noah reached over and held Kristan. "You know, I didn't do that on purpose. I was as scared as you. I wanted it to be so perfect I forgot the one thing to make it that."

"I know. I know because I know you. You are that kind of guy. That's why I didn't even ask. I knew you would protect us."

"Thank you."

"Noah, tomorrow will be perfect. We'll get sunshine, dinner, music, and sex. Safe sex."

"You mean we still have tomorrow?"

"Yes. That's a promise."

Chapter 9. Saying Goodbye

After a quick run on the beach Noah returned to make Kristan breakfast in bed. He was bound and determined to have a better go at things today. The condoms were placed in the bathroom and at the bedside so he wouldn't forget. He even had them next to his car keys and put one inside Kristan's purse. He'd picked a flower and put it in a tiny vase and brought it to her with the bacon and eggs which included a flaky croissant par honey. The orange and strawberries added bright color to the plate and all he could do was smile. She was his princess today and tomorrow. He didn't know about the rest of his life but right now he felt wonderfully in control. Damn last night.

"For you," he said as he walked in the bedroom. The curtain had been opened and the sun poured in. He set down the breakfast tray right next to her in the bed. "You are beautiful. And today is our day."

"I know. It's going to be glorious." First she took a big drink of the juice, then started on the crisp bacon and eggs.

"There's more if you need it."

She sucked on the strawberry before eating all of it. "Tell me about getting into your college choice."

I selected four to apply to and I've heard back from two. I'll let you know when I get the one I really want."

"Sure. I bet you get into all of them. Then it will be difficult to make that choice."

"Let's just say none are down here. We won't be near each other next year."

"And so we won't talk about it until it happens." Kristan was just fine with that, she knew they both needed to move on. Wasn't she going to do that on the way back or the day before?

The pair went swimming in the ocean. The waves were big and brilliant today crashing near the shore bringing the salt water and ocean tide way up early in the morning. By two o'clock the tide was out on this beautiful Saturday. Noah and Kristan never thought about last night only what was before them. They made a reservation for a steakhouse that had seafood too. It showcased a singer in the piano bar.

After being on the beach all day the couple took a nap before the special evening. Kristan checked her phone and responded to Taylor who asked how things were going. Her mom asked her to send pictures, so she sent a few beach pics from earlier. In the kitchen she poured one of her little white wine bottles into a glass and sat out on the porch overlooking the beach. This was a beautiful place. "I could live here."

"Me too. Looking at that every day would make your mood over the top good before you went to work."

"You are going to be flying airplanes. You will see everything, every day!"

"Never thought about it like that. I only see the instruments and what they tell me."

"I suppose. Are you sure though?"

"It's like the sky is there and you control it, never letting it control you. I'm more into the workings of piloting and not the scenery as yet. Does that make sense?"

Kristan looked at Noah. He was going to be a super pilot someday. What guy wouldn't be nervous about sex? She guessed the first time was more sophisticated or tense than flying a plane. She smirked a bit then laughed out loud.

"What's funny?"

"Nothing really. I think you are ready for next year."

"I think so too. But first tonight."

The restaurant was the fanciest Kristan had ever been to while at the beach. They were treated like a prince and princess. They both ordered steak and lobster, would share an appetizer and dessert. The waiter offered them a wine list and brought them each a glass of cabernet with their meal. The piano singer was fabulous, adding to the whole experience. Many tunes they recognized, others not so much. Kristan wore her prom dress and Noah had his suit jacket on with khakis. The pair definitely looked like they were mid-twenties. Maybe they were just for a night. There was no one to tell them no, or to go home. It was a special night and the aura around them added to it. Just for a moment when she was drinking the wine Kristan thought about her mother and how she didn't get to be with her brand new husband on their wedding night. It would have felt like this-a special feeling with someone you love, even if hers was not forever. Noah thought Kristan looked especially happy tonight. He leaned over and took her hand and held it. Then he kissed it. He did love her, right now he loved her. The waiter brought the dessert, a chocolate cake with a mousse topping. Delicious.

The couple left the restaurant and made their way back to the condo. Kristan leaned over in the car and kissed Noah, over and over. Both were feeling a bit heady.

Once inside Noah turned the music on, Kristan lit a candle, and the two of them danced in the living room with the glass door open and curtains billowing in and out from the ocean winds. The most perfect night that could be had was had by two young adults in mutual consent. Memories made that would last a lifetime.

Around three in the morning Noah went to the bathroom to retrieve the third and final condom for the night. He smiled at himself. Lucky for him after twenty four hours he had this sex thing figured out. Kristan looked like she was pretty happy herself. Both would sleep in tomorrow. Sweet dreams. Kristan got up, blew out the candle and shut the sliding door. They both pulled up the covers and fell asleep happy and worn out. The moon was full this weekend and tonight the light poured in as it had reached high in the sky over top of them. It seemed to light up the whole beach, and make the ocean which had completely calmed, silvery. Noah thought this place was awesome and couldn't get any better.

Kristan and Noah did sleep in but when they awoke they were famished. "I'm buying breakfast today. Where shall we go?"

"I think we need one of those all night places that serve breakfast all day. Something like a Waffle House."

"That's a fabulous idea. And then what?"

"Breakfast. Walk. Read. Pool. Bike ride." Noah listed off everything he could think of.

"Sounds like a plan. Maybe a golf cart ride too. You are cooking dinner tonight right?"

"Yes, I am. I'm making you the best BBQ this side of Carolina aka Carolina style."

"Oh my, where did you learn?"

"My mother taught me." He laughed and gave her a wink.

"I love BBQ, especially Carolina style. Vinegar is my fave. Yum."

"Okay, then, settled. Waffle House first."

On the way Kristan decided she would wait until the walk to deliver any bad news. That seemed like a better idea.

And so the day rolled on from one thing to the next. The walk turned out not to be the bummer that Kristan thought it might be. She couldn't believe her ears.

"Kristan honey, I know we love each other and that we just made love, over and over, but I also know that we will be very far apart. I don't feel like living to only wait on your every move. My mother lives without her husband and I live without my father. It's okay.

Seriously, why grieve all the time? Just get on with living. I don't think that we should feel sorry that we cannot be around each other. That's like always wanting what you can't have. We can be friends, special friends, and someday, when school is done if one of us feels like calling the other then just do it. But if one has found someone else then that's the way it goes too. What do you think?"

"I think, Noah, that is, well, like so grown up. Where did you get so intelligent? I guess you've lived with death and apartness where most of us haven't. Except my mom, she has and she recovered."

"I suppose so." Noah reflected. "Your mom paints it away and found love again. And she has you."

"You know what? It's like saying goodbye without really saying goodbye. Friends is a great way to part, wishing each other well with happy feelings going forward is a good thing."

"And we could text or call if we need to talk to know the other one is okay."

And with that the walk came to an end. The couple hugged each other. It wasn't relief. It was joy in knowing one another and the freedom to pursue the future. Kristan thought this whole man relationship thing was going quite well. Maybe she was growing up. Being away from high school was surely a good thing. Possibly she was just lucky. She didn't like playing games and this seemed to happen naturally. The breakup was much easier than she ever thought it would be. No tears on either side. Yes. All was good.

Noah prepped the BBQ to cook slowly all day while they read, went to the pool, and later hopped on some bikes and pedaled under some huge Live Oak trees. Kristan made a cherry pie to go with the vanilla ice cream she had remembered to buy.

Later that night they had goodbye sex. And it was good. Maybe they would miss this. After all they just got together. But Kristan said, "No. We can't do that. These memories are what we have. We can text but no future dates until after you graduate high school."

That settled it. They slept. They drove back both in a quiet mode listening to the radio. It was okay.

"I had the best weekend, Noah. I'll always remember it. Forever."

"I did too. You gave me your heart and mind and I love that. I just can't tie you down, or myself, while I hopefully go to Colorado next year."

"I know."

"Even if it is somewhere else, things will still be the same. Let's concentrate on who we want to become."

"Yes. We are only young once, etc. etc." She said it but some sadness set in.

Noah gave her hand a squeeze. When they arrived to her dorm. He got out and took her things upstairs, then said goodbye. He hugged her hard. She hugged back. It would be okay.

"I'll text you when I get home so you know I made it."

"Yes. Thanks again. I had the best time with you, the dinner, your awesome BBQ, the beach, us."

"I did too. You are fabulous and beautiful. Have a great time in college, learn so you can get ahead in anything."

"You do the same." She kissed him one last time on the lips. She smiled.

He winked and then was gone. She went into her room and called Taylor. It was time for some girl talk.

Jeremy texted and said a big group was meeting at a bar to watch Monday night football. Would she like to come?

Of course, yes! That night she sat with new friends getting over an old friend after having a super weekend. How can life be so good all at once? That sounded like a question for Professor Knox. She tucked that in the back of her mind as the freshman students sat at a large table ordering beer, shots, and pizza with a few wings all while watching professional football. They chatted about next Saturday's college game and where the parties might be.

Parent's weekend came up and discussions of who and where to go for dinner. Thanksgiving wasn't too far behind. Her mother called and said that she and her father would be going to Paris, and that she should go to her uncles for the week. Take someone with you if you like, you know they love company. They lived near the beach in Savannah. Later on she found out that Levi's mother was going to visit her sister in Texas and that he didn't have to go. Kristan immediately asked him if he wanted to come with her for the week. She knew it would be okay with her uncles as they had a massive home, or mansion, with hired help. And just like that life moved on.

Chapter 10. Parents Weekend

Kristan thought about her perfect weekend at the beach. The thought made her smile. But Parents Weekend had arrived! She couldn't wait to show her parents where everything was located and introduce them to Jeremy along with a few other friends. She felt like she was in this limbo land kind of place, wanting their love and affection by showing them she could do adult stuff. But wait-she couldn't show them her new found skills like drinking and cavorting with the opposite sex. No way.

She was ready to have conversations about worldly things, newsworthy and important to the world's future. Her school work and grades were up to her and there would be no phone calls if she did poorly. Not that that ever happened to her, but she knew of friends in high school that had to take summer courses every year just to go on to the next level. She felt sorry for them.

Kristan looked out her dorm window and saw her parent's car. Right on time. She ran down to meet them grabbing her leather purse. She had dressed up for dinner. Dinner would be early at some place downtown. Not at the club place, but some place with southern dishes that seemed to be quite popular. Her parents were dressed up as well. They got in the car after greetings with hellos and hugs. Kristan proceeded to point out every building known to her.

"You seem to know the school quite well after a couple of months."

"Mom, of course, we walk it every day."

"Have you made any more friends from the sorority?" her father asked.

"Yes, we've done a couple of service days on the weekends to help with the community."

"Like what?"

"Like clean up the parks and make food at the local shelter."

"You cooked in a kitchen?" her mom asked. She turned to look at her in the back seat of the car.

"It was quite easy, in fact, because everything is labeled in the fridge with clear and easy directions. We worked as a team. Actually, it was fun like running our own restaurant."

"I'm impressed," said her dad. He smiled at her in the rear view mirror.

They circled around a few times looking at the club and restaurants. It was an old town that seemed to having a new renaissance of sorts. Maybe the university was expanding and they needed to upgrade the downtown so the students had a place to hang out. Chloe didn't understand. If one was underage why have bars in college towns? It seemed like an oxymoron. When she grew up one could drink beer at eighteen, later they raised the age, except for the military which recruits at eighteen.

"I don't understand how one can go to war at eighteen but cannot drink a beer while they eat pizza. They know they are drinking; let's be realistic."

"Mom, you're right but I don't make the laws."

"Speaking of laws, remember that fight out at the quarry which ended with the Rebekka woman dead from a gunshot? The one we recently talked about?"

"Vaguely."

"Well, her twin sister is running to be a congresswoman."

"What? Seriously?"

"Yes. It is the truth. Good for her. She wants to work on women's labor issues and women and children, among many other things like the health of the ocean, healthcare, and renewable energies."

"Great. Doesn't she live in our neighborhood?"

"She does. She's been overseas in the air force these past couple years. She's made a name for herself. Too bad about her sister."

"She started a nonprofit to help young women that are displaced and not ready to be out on their own. The age group is very fragile, especially if they don't have jobs and are away from their parents. Many don't have parents that can parent and are not in college."

"Sounds good."

"The church used to provide places like that but I don't think they are involved anymore."

"Okay let's go in before the crowd arrives," said Richard.

The place was already packed. Not even elbow room at the bar. Chloe looked all around. She was excited to be out in some new place she'd never been before. The hostess asked for their names and said, "It will be awhile down here but I can seat you upstairs on the second floor right away."

"Perfect. We'll follow," said Richard.

Up a long and winding staircase they climbed. There was a bar out back but they kept climbing. Another small bar lay at the top of the stairs. Then the hostess led them forward towards the windows to a large old room. It was semi fixed up, plain, classic and with assorted items from old times on the walls. The pictures were hung with ribbons like something out of the twenties. Chloe loved it!

"Oh my, this reminds me of Paris in some of the older restaurants. I feel like I'm in Paris. But here I am."

"Here you are mother, right in Vista, Georgia. The rural south plains with nothing but red dirt, palmettos and large white oaks," said Kristan.

"What? You been reading about the ole south?"

"You have to admit for miles and miles there's nothing. There's the beach, there's college and then I-75." Kristan smiled. She had no idea what she herself was talking about.

Her mother stared at her just a bit. Must be this old building, maybe there's some ghost in here haunting us. "This building certainly has a history, some good and some not so good, I reckon." Chloe looked around.

"That is the thing, buildings and trees, these things that last have seen what went on in the Deep South. They have the firsthand knowledge. We just read about it and are not sure of the accuracy." Richard gave Kristan his thoughts aloud.

"Thank goodness times have changed. More civility is always needed," Kristan expounded. Once again she wasn't sure why she added that. There was a certain awareness going on around campus at the moment. Maybe it was that. Possibly it was a sadness for our history. Did we know the truth? She liked her college and everyone was super nice. This had to a part of growing up and being away at college. One began to think like an adult. That's it. She put it to rest and looked at the menu.

The waitress arrived and took drink orders. It was rather fancy up here and all. Kristan ordered a white claw, which was her usual, a seltzer water with alcohol. Chloe and Richard ordered a martini. Bread was served in a warm basket, waters put forth and plates removed, napkins laid across ones lap and the candles lit.

"I'm going to order the duck!" exclaimed Chloe.

"Mother, you're so excited. Kristan's eyes rolled wide and she looked at her dad.

"Once your mother had pheasant with Russian vodkas, so I expect now she wants what she never had: duck." He acknowledged his wife. "I'm getting scallops."

"Are you ready to order?" asked the waitress.

"We are. I'll have the duck with blue cheese grits and fried green tomatoes from the appetizer list. White wine, house is fine. But first another cosmopolitan."

"And for you ma'am?"

"I'd like the Steel Magnolias Shrimp and Grits with smoked gouda grits. It sounds delish."

"You will like that. Anything more to drink?"

"No thank you. I'm fine. Maybe an expresso after dinner."

"And you Sir. What will you have?"

"I'd like the scallops with pasta and mushrooms."

"Is the butternut squash oaky as well?"

"Yes. Fine. I'll have another martini, please."

The waitress explained about the buildings upstairs being a dress shop back in the day. It sat idle for many years. They cleaned it up as the university needed to add more to its downtown when Vista was growing. She didn't know if there were any ghosts but she wouldn't say that there wasn't any. She winked.

"You know Kristan, I thought we were supposed to go to Magenta Fleurs for dinner."

"Yes. But this looked so nice. We will go there for lunch tomorrow."

The music played and the family enjoyed one another in a brand new setting. This was a whole new thing: three grownups no more child, sitting together in some old store in the middle of nowhere, and relaxing to the heartbeat of playing a new song in South Georgia. One can't protect their children forever even though they'd like to. Memories is what would live on now, promises made, promises kept and the uncertainty of the future. It would be up to the three of them filling the pail, painting the scene, or traveling a new road. Someday they might be at a new restaurant sharing the second or third act. Timeless. That is how the evening felt to Chloe, Richard and their dear daughter Kristan. For Kristan the world was beautiful like a picture with so many new frames exposed.

Momma Chloe took pictures with her phone before dessert. She felt mesmerized like back in time to Paris and this made her feel jubilant if only for an evening.

The next morning ...

Chloe texted Kristan ...Wear something warm it's chilly outside.

Kristan texted back ... Thanks. Will do. Boots too!

Chloe and Kristan drove to Magenta Fleurs, which happened to be a floral shop with an attached café. The coolness outside was welcomed after a hot summer of unrelenting heat and humidity. First they purchased a Starbucks chai tea latte and iced mocha cappuccino and drove around campus looking at all the magnificent trees and buildings made of red brick. It was an extremely beautiful campus and with the moss swaying made it even prettier like a girl with long hair blowing in the breeze. This made Chloe a bit jealous that she never had this opportunity to be at such a lovely place. Then again she had Paris. She'd studied under tutors and stayed in her one room apartment. Paris was like one giant university. Now that her daughter was here she wanted to feel what Kristan was feeling. Kristan turned up the music and pointed in the direction of downtown.

"It says turn at Magnolia Place, then it's the third store on the right."

"Okay, I see it."

They parked the car and headed towards the flower shop. "I wonder why my professor recommended this place."

"Did he?"

"Welcome. Please come in!" A lady ushered them in the store after opening the door for them.

"Thank you."

Chloe and Kristan walked in and looked around. It was a flower shop filled with magenta colored floral pictures on the walls. Magenta Fleurs. She guessed hence the name of the place.

"Very pretty, unusual."

"Please look around. If you are here for lunch it is through that entryway." The woman pointed to the left side of the flower shop.

"Yes. Thank you. Again." said Chloe.

The ladies went next door and found a table in the small café style, old-world looking restaurant. Kristan had that ah ha moment when she looked at the menu. There were flowers in the food.

"I suppose here is your answer," said Chloe, also looking over the menu.

"And up there, too." Kristan looked up above the small fireplace over to her left.

Two deer heads, one with large antlers and the other with none, were stuffed above the mantel and hung on the wall. The women smiled at one another. This didn't bother them. They thought them rather regal but some people nowadays disliked animal heads placed anywhere. Times were changing but appreciating how far we have come with everything in life made them feel good about where they each were in their own life. This particular model from the past didn't displace them or make them feel ashamed. For that is how the world worked and hunters hunted animals for food.

"What do you think of our antlers?" asked the waitress.

"They are beautiful. Looks like a father and child," explained Kristan.

"I believe it is, back in the day before they made it illegal to kill the young. I don't know what to think of it. Some people hate it. It disgusts them, others are fine. I guess we are all different in our tastes of life. Now what'll you have for lunch?" Such simple words but the waitress had managed to solve the world's problems in a paragraph. Good for her thought Chloe we need wise people roaming around doing everyday business.

"We'll have the Champagne with Hibiscus to start." Chloe ordered.

"Sandwiches or soup, or both?"

"I'll have the grilled cheese and tomato soup," ordered Kristan.

"And I'll have the chicken salad on croissant with wild rice mushroom soup."

"Go ahead and order dessert as it comes with the meal."

"Chocolate Cake with Lavender for me!" Kristan cried out.

"For me the Peach Crisp with Lavender."

"I'll leave one menu here for you to check out the history of the color magenta."

"The history of magenta?" asked Kristan.

"It says here there is no wavelength for the color of magenta. Our eyes want to see it as a blend of red and blue but it actually doesn't exist."

"Really?" Kristan had never heard that. "What?"

"Apparently, they named it after a town in Italy from some battle." Chloe paused and breathed out rather forcefully drawing Kristan's attention. She stared at her mother and remembered the poem. The blood.

"Yes. I know this color well and it's not a figment of my imagination. It exists."

The ladies drank the Hibiscus Champagne which had a pinch of cranberry tart to it, ate their sandwiches and soup (flowerless) in quiet, and then took bites of the dessert.

"I'm going to eat the lavender!"

Smiling now the brocade of death was broken.

"Me too!"

Kristan and her mom left the restaurant and on the way out the door ran into the sister of Rebekka, the dead woman from back home. Chloe recognized her but it had been a long time.

"Hello, Mrs. Lindemann."

"Hello."

"Kim."

"Kim, it's been a long time. Please call me Chloe."

"Chloe."

"How are you? This is my daughter Kristan. She's at college down here. It's her first year."

"Nice to meet you Kristan. And I'm fine. I've just returned to the states and things are very busy."

"I heard you might run to be a congresswoman. How wonderful!"

"Yes. But first I'm starting a foundation to help women. That's why I'm down here."

"Great. I wish you luck. I'm so sorry about your sister."

"Thank you. She could have used a place like the one I'm opening. She felt lost."

"Good for you. Let me know what I can do to help."

"Thank you."

"What city?"

"The home will be in Savannah. I'm working on that right now. Also, another place but that has tight security measures so I cannot talk about that one."

"Well. I read about cyber-crimes increasing in the headlines today. Hopefully, our services are all over that one." Chloe wasn't sure why she added that extra tidbit but she watched Kim to see if she wavered and she did.

"Here's my card if you ever need me or want to donate to the cause."

"Thank you. I will."

"Nice to meet you Kristan and good luck at Vista."

"You too. And best for your ventures, especially running for congress," Kristan said.

The rest of the weekend flew by and just like that Kristan was saying goodbye to her parents.

"I had a wonderful time honey. Keep up the good work and remember to call your uncles and let them know you'll be coming for Thanksgiving and bringing a guest with you."

"Will do. Should I take them something?"

"Sure, like wine or champagne? If your fake ID doesn't buy that then try a Christmas tree ornament. You can help them cook the turkey dinner I'm sure."

"Okay, bye. Have fun in Europe. Text pictures or Facetime." She hugged and waved them goodbye.

Chapter 11). Saint Mary's

"Thanks so much for coming with me Levi. We are going to have a blast. My uncles are the greatest. Get ready for a good time!" Kristan drove her mother's navy blue SUV towards I-75.

"Which way do you want to go?"

"Anyway you want to get there. I'll drive when you need me to, okay?'

"Sure but north or south, do you have a preference?'

"South, go south."

"Sounds like a plan. We go I-75 to I-10 east, then I-95 north to St. Mary's Road, then we take the Cumberland Island Ferry and they'll drop us at my uncle's dock." She'd memorized the trip. She'd been there before. It always brought back the fondest of memories. Martin was her favorite uncle. Actually, he was her mother's brother and she only had one uncle. He married a man named Thomas years ago and the two of them made sure she always had a great time. Kristan thought everyone should have gay uncles in their life. They were colorful, artistic, fun and loved to cook. She was thinking about the delicious food her and Levi were going to be served for a whole week. She smiled.

"What are you thinking about with that smile on your face? Noah?" he asked.

"You are funny! I told you it's over. We broke up."

"Possibly, though, he still makes you smile."

"No. Seriously not. I am thinking about all the homemade food we are going to be served. My uncles do not have kids and they love to treat me like a princess. So you will be the prince for a week. Can you handle it?"

"Sure. But you know I can help cook as I work at The Bean Dip. Even though I wait tables they put me on the grill quite often." Levi explained.

"Likely they will teach you some new recipes. The kitchen is the place to be. I did tell you they own a mansion, right?"

"Yes, I think you did. Do you mean we can get lost in the house?"

"Lost for week if you wanted to."

"As long as we can find the kitchen we'll survive!" Levi seemed excited for this trip. He really hadn't been many places in life. His mother was single, still living in Baton Rouge, working as a waitress living in a three room apartment with a community bathroom in a hallway that leads to the other apartment. She couldn't afford anything more. She also had two more children much younger than Levi. But she told him to go follow his dreams. She borrowed money from one of her customers that liked her, and for a few favors now and then, her kid was going to college. Maybe he'd remember her someday and come looking for her and help her just a bit. If not, that was okay too. He wanted to be an oceanographer so he headed east towards the Atlantic Ocean and enrolled in Vista University. He found a job at a local restaurant through her contacts and lived in a room rented from an elderly lady who lost her husband. Everything seemed to be in place. He wasn't coming home for Thanksgiving as he had an invitation to go with a fellow classmate, not a girlfriend, to a place near the ocean. Little did he know he was going to be on the ocean.

Levi had a head full of curly light brown hair, lean body build and a smile to go with his gregarious loud laugh. Kristan was relieved he was coming along. He said his mother would completely understand and wanted him to gain experiences that he wasn't afforded in his prior life. Kristan suspected that maybe he was poor. It didn't matter in college as everyone was the same. There wasn't anything to prove. Equal was equal. But she could tell he really wanted to go with her and gain an experience. She was happy to oblige this small opportunity for growth, family and the experience of a culinary holiday.

"My maps says two and a half hours. Not long at all." Levi stated.

"But the ferry boat adds an hour," Kristan remembered, "so three and a half hours, and with a stop, make it four hours."

"Not bad. Let me know when you want me to drive."

Kristan felt like she was on an adventure. Usually she spent Thanksgiving with her parents at the house. Her mother made the dinner or they went out to a nice place. Here she was going to her uncles for a whole week. They'd be fishing, boating, cooking, hunting, quailing, or visiting the local artists in town she suspected. They also had about ten dogs, three cats, and numerous chickens which hatched fresh eggs. Their home was definitely in a unique area, one could get lost she reminded herself. She couldn't remember if it was called a swamp, bayou, or national refuge area. Her uncles would give her and Levi the full history lesson, so no worries. She would need to go to town where the cell tower was to call her mother in Europe. In town they could browse the art work for Christmas gifts and get any items they might need that they forgot to pack.

Kristan played music from her selections and rolled down the highway towards I-10.

Three hours later they were boarding the ferry boat for the trip to Cumberland Island, only the two of them were departing to a dock that belonged to a house off the cul de sac down from Thomas Ale Road, which was the last dock before you hit the island where ponies and horses ran free. Incredible is what Levi thought. He couldn't wait to see that sight.

"I think maybe I should fill you in on my uncles with just a quick review of their backgrounds. Just so your jaw doesn't drop or your eyeball gets dislodged." She laughed.

"Seriously, like what are they? Weird, ugly, or what?'

"No, no. Just the highlights. For instance Thomas was a priest before he got married. I suppose that complicates everything, just saying. And he's like super rich with family money inherited from beer making, though, he doesn't disclose the details. Martin was married to a lady before and had several serious girlfriends-so he's a late gay, I suspect. Martin has worked all over the world in many countries, serving the poor and hungry, with building houses and making food through gardens and livestock. They both love to fish, they'll teach you to catch 'em, fillet 'em, prepare 'em and cook them. They are working on their hunting skills, and they paint and play the piano, sing too."

"Seriously, all that? My we may never leave. Maybe we should spend summer vacations here." He expanded the proposed hospitality.

"You know that would be a great idea. Maybe we should suggest it to them for next summer. But let's see how this visit goes first."

"Yes. For sure. What's your major for college again?"

"Mine? Nursing. But it's difficult to get in so I may have to change it to another field. What's yours again, I forgot?"

"Oceanography."

"How on earth did you select oceanography?"

"Baton Rouge is near the gulf but I kept dreaming of the big ocean. I love swimming. I suppose I combined the two. I did watch National Geographic and saw a few episodes of the late Jacques Cousteau. That did it."

"Well, come to think of it, maybe you are in the right place. There's a heck of a lot of water around here all headed out to the Atlantic. Look over there," Kristan points to the outlet near Cumberland Island. They were aboard the ferry and seated. They left the car at the dock for the week. Her uncles had golf carts, bicycles, and motorbikes, in addition to boats and jet skis.

It was Saturday before Thanksgiving. Likely they would come back to the mainland on Wednesday before the feast to browse in the art shops, etc. before spending four more days over at the mansion. Soon they would be there.

Quickly they loaded onto the private dock and the ferry pushed away to take the other quests to Cumberland Island for camping and observing the feral horses.

Kristan and Levi picked up their suitcases and other belongings and headed off the dock. No sooner had they begun walking when someone driving a golf cart came toward them waving voraciously, calling out "Darlings ... I'm coming!"

"Thomas, we're here. We made it." Kristan recognized her uncle Thomas.

"Look at you both. How wonderful. We are ecstatic that you are gracing us with your selves for a whole week. My, oh my, we are going to treat you like royals." He smiled and waved his hand around and around. He loaded them onto the golf cart and then sprang into action doing a few circles himself in a giddy sort of fashion. Yes. Thomas was the alpha female in the relationship if that meant anything. He was flamboyant, extravagant, and especially cordial.

"Onto the castle," Kristan and Levi were all smiles. Yep, this was going to be an experience!

Hiding behind the shrubbery and taller trees, past the new growth oaks, was a swimming pool. He pulled the golf cart right up next to the pool and then through the portico to the side of the mansion. This was near the kitchen. "You can unload here and go inside, Martin will take you to your rooms. Rest up for a few minutes, return and we'll take you both for a tour of the outside before afternoon sets in. Just to show you where everything is located and what you can do around here all week."

"Come in. Welcome. I'm Martin and you must be Levi. Thank you so much for coming all this way. And look at my little niece, Kristan, you look fabulous! But of course you have the best mother in all the world. Beautiful, loving, kind and centuries-old longstanding wisdom given to her by our almighty father, Lord Jesus Christ."

"Martin, you are so kind yourself and full of compliments like none other anywhere. Mother would love all of those. Thank you."

"Let's get you to your rooms. There is sixteen rooms in the main house and four out back near the pool. We have a guest cottage with two rooms but that hasn't been used in many years. We also have a small barn for our three horses and chickens and Thomas is building a brick one room distillery for making homemade beer, maybe even whiskey. Ha ha."

"Busy. Busy. Will we have homemade beer for Thanksgiving?"

"Possibly." Martin took the couple upstairs and found them their rooms. The rooms were separated by a bathroom towards the front of the mansion.

"I can't wait to look at all these paintings on the walls." Kristan looked down both hallways on the second level. "Are they your paintings?"

"Yes. Look at them tomorrow. I'll tell you about them. First up, settle in, then come downstairs and we'll take you outside before dinner to see what you can do all week."

It had been a couple years since Kristan had been here and the uncles had done quite a lot of work. The pool was added, the paintings, the pool house and who knows what else. Maybe they even had a wine cellar she thought.

"Kristan, this is a palace."

"I know, right?!" She glanced around her room and noticed all the intricacies from beaded and fringed curtains, to French style Louis the XI bed linens and pillows, and antique quality dressers and nightstands. The adorable settee below the window beckoned her body to come sit, relax, and look out the window towards the long extended driveway. I guess you could have a car here if you wanted. Maybe it was for the horses. Was there a carriage? It all seemed surreal-then again, her uncles fit right in with this extravagance. This week was going to be beyond fun. It would downright outrageous! Who knows maybe some out of town guests were flying in on the private runway?

"Children," he shouted up the stairs. "Time for play."

Levi and Kristan came quickly with apologies that they were just taking it all in.

"Outside we go. We want to show you our southern ocean view." Martin directed them outside near the pool where he had refreshments set out just for them. "Grab something of your choosing and hop on. Thomas, time to go!"

Thomas appeared from behind the tall shrubs with smiles of delight. "I'm ready!"

"Let's roll," said Martin, "wait that sounds too airplanish, or deadly. Let's hit it." he hit the pedal and off they went to survey the grounds, all twenty acres of it. Martin was always impeccably dressed in long sleeved shirts, pressed and with a vest. He wore coordinated slacks and shoes. Occasionally he had a thrill shirt on when he painted, which was often. His hair was black with small curls combed back and he appeared cleanly shaven. He was shorter than Thomas.

"My grandfather's uncle owned all the land here-about three miles long and a mile wide all in front of the big island. We were between Cumberland and Saint Mary's. There's quite some history there with the Spaniards and settlers and later the bootleggers. I'll tell you more later this week. Our property extends over this whole point. Pretty nice, I think. Though someday it might be nice to have a few neighbors. What do you think?" Thomas was a pleasant fellow with longer blondish brown hair. He stood tall, Roman like. But his mood was always light, musical and mischievous. If it wasn't for Martin he might never have achieved such success with his companies he inherited. Martin was good for Thomas.

"I like it private. Invite people over when you want them, otherwise the castle is yours."

"Levi, you got a point. Invite them when you want them."

"We love it here. So much to do all the time." Martin drove them around and showed them the boats, the keys, life vests, fishing poles and bait, and reminded them to take sandwiches and beverages from the kitchen. He showed them the garden, the mini forest of trees, pointed out to the swampland beyond, the guesthouse near the water's edge, and even a small beach with sand. There was a fire pit, a putting hole, and small barn. In the barn was kittens and hay, art supplies to paint whatever you wanted, and a four-wheeler. Saddles and stirrups and sets of reins for riding were present.

"How do you take care of all this?" Kristan asked.

"We do have four helpers, or servants, that work for us. But they do stay out of the way and enjoy their jobs very much. You'll see them. One takes care of the horses, boats, and jet skis and other sports, another tends the gardens and lawn, shrubs, etc., a third does the cooking and supplies when we don't, and finally, the maid who cleans our precious castle is the best."

"Must cost a fortune, then again, this place must have cost more than that." Levi was imagining the impossible.

"Well, Levi I inherited the land, a few companies and my cohort here has worked hard his whole life. I guess he saved a small fortune. Good man that is." Thomas gave some input.

"Both of you have done well. May we be lucky as well," Kristan proposed a small toast to good fortune.

Martin kept going about the grounds after the stables and showed them some special gardens, mostly floral, that was dead now for the semi winter. It was November and things looked a bit bleak, darker, and wintrier like. Martin said they would pick up the turkey on Wednesday and asked did the two want to go to town then? That sounded fine. He said they should play, go fishing, boating, riding and wander about. They might even see the horses from this side. Dinner was at seven every night after cocktails. Were they old enough for cocktails? They replied yes, because they were college students.

The sun could be seen setting on the south western lawn every night. Then it was time for drinks, dinner, and a nightly fire inside at the grand fireplace. Martin and Thomas were especially glad the pair had made the trip. They enlisted them to help make the dinner on Thursday, as the cook was off with Monday and Tuesday night as well.

Chapter 12). Uncles Castle

Kristan and Levi went fishing on Monday morning using the stables servant on the boat as a backup. That way they were able to enjoy the sport and not worry about the navigation. The pair decided that Friday they would take the boat out themselves for a pleasure cruise, not navigating too far from the castle homestead. She actually showed them where they could go and to use the depth finder at all times. This would secure a pleasant trip out in the swamp (marsh) or ocean. The area was pretty with the sun melting on the still water and seagulls flying in all directions. If they caught a few fish they'd prep and prepare them to serve with the homemade beer as an appetizer on Thursday. It was a fun day escaping and the sun and sport tired them out. Pizza was for dinner, homemade of course, and both went to bed early forgoing the drinks and fireside chats this Monday night.

On Tuesday stormy weather woke the travelers up earlier than usual. Kristan grabbed her robe and made her way downstairs to the kitchen. She poured a cup of coffee and returned to the second floor where she found Levi perusing the hallway, staring at the paintings done by Martin. Slowly he made his way down one side and back the opposite wall. Each painting had a frame and was rather large, maybe 50" X 30", or four feet by two and a half feet. In addition to the portraits were other paintings of seascapes, trees, as well as buildings, old buildings like churches or museums. One painting looked like a house down in the Caribbean with white columns, plantation style, as is usually noted in Greek architecture.

"Beautiful. He's very good," said Levi.

"Do you think so?"

"Yes, come look at all of them."

"Where do I start?"

"Begin at my door here and head this way, return when you've hit the window and come back the other way. Then from the staircase we'll check the other wing. We can look together, okay?" Levi instructed.

Levi sat on the hallway settee and waited. He checked his phone, no calls. He tried to get service but the uncles had told him he may have to go out back by the pool to make a call.

Kristan drank her coffee and studied each painting. There was much detail. Most were oil paintings she guessed but a couple were watercolor, she could tell as she had dabbled in that during art class. She wondered if the people he had painted, sat and waited patiently, or he used an old photo and performed this artistic expression in his studio. She'd have to ask him that question.

"You made it. Quite nice wouldn't you say?" Levi asked.

"For certain, such talent. I wonder if he has sold any or presented to an art gallery."

"I don't know but you know what they say all artists are starving artists."

"Isn't that a shame? People should see these paintings. Are all creatives starving artists?" Kristan asked.

"Oh, that is one dystopian thought. Maybe depressed people should go to art galleries and read books, then they will get out of themselves and undo the cycle." Levi contemplated.

"What a simplistic thing to say but you sound quite right," said Kristan.

"Why do you think I picked oceanography?" Levi asked.

Kristan stared at Levi and she didn't know what to say.

"I don't really know either, except looking at these paintings makes me think the sea has a treasure trove of beauty, untouched with buried treasure. I seek the unknown," he surprised himself.

"Let's finish the hallway and get some breakfast. I want to walk all over this place and discover something new. We have to help with dinner tonight."

"Yes. I wonder what that is. Something French, I'm certain."

On their walk Kristan told Levi all about her mother and the past, even a little more about her high school boyfriend. She enjoyed talking with him and she felt he enlisted her as a friend as well.

Upon returning to the kitchen Martin and Thomas sat at the table looking over a French cookbook and writing a few recipes down.

"Look who's here! The two of you look absolutely provincial like a prince and princess!" Thomas exclaimed.

"But we aren't my sweet uncles, we are friends. We are becoming very good friends, I think," stated Kristan.

"I agree to that."

"That is a mighty fine thing to have. Friendship. Individuals that will pull you through much of life's torments, sadness, and atrocities," said Martin in dramatic fashion.

"Okay, enough. Who is ready to prep the food for making dinner later?'

"Levi, can you do the prep? I would like to take a nap after our ten mile walk."

"I would love to," he replied.

Kristan went to take a nap in her ginormous bed. Must be all the fresh air she thought before falling fast asleep. Meanwhile, Levi helped prep the rabbit and quail, which he had never eaten either before in his life. What an experience! He was so glad he was here learning something new and with a good friend meeting new people. They prepped a few vegetable dishes, set them in the refrigerator, and then made a bacon wrapped scallop appetizer and a pear tart for dessert. One wondered silently if the uncles ate like this all the time.

"In case you are wondering we do eat like this all the time. One week a month we don't plan and we eat dinner for breakfast, breakfast for dinner, or go out every night, even take out fast food if on the mainland." Martin explained.

Levi didn't know what to believe. Was that the truth? He couldn't be sure.

"I'm kidding!" Martin and Levi laughed out loud, repeatedly, one sounding like the other. Thomas walked in the room and looked at both of them. He wasn't sure who was laughing because he knows Martins laugh after all these years but he heard a similar laugh from Levi, or did he?

"What is so funny?"

"Nothing really, just that I told him we eat like this all the time," Martin explained.

Another explosion of laughs filled the room. Martin didn't notice but Thomas did.

Kristan woke to laughter from the downstairs kitchen. She heard her uncle Martin and Levi laughing about something. The kind of laughter you have when you can't stop. She'd get Levi to tell her the joke later. Time to go play some pool since it was still stormy outside.

Maybe Friday, or even Thanksgiving morning they could go riding horses. Possibly her uncles would like that. She knew Wednesday was reserved for the mainland.

Tuesday's dinner was fabulous and credit was given to Levi. "Levi, you are a good cook in addition to your student oceanography studies. Maybe you will specialize in seafood someday." Thomas was handing out the compliments.

"Maybe. The dishes were fun to make. I totally enjoyed myself and lost thought of any school or tests, even homework."

"More French wine Kristan?"

"Please, I love it. You can help me with the taste testing and how to do that."

While Thomas showed Kristan how to taste test wine from anywhere, Martin and Levi talked about his paintings.

"How did you ever paint so many people? Each one is special, very unique. Did the people sit for you or did you use a photo?"

"That is a great question and the answer is both. Most of them are my previous loves, places I've visited, or homes

I've lived in. That is what makes them unique-they are all my loves." Martin's eyes danced when he spoke. Levi thought he was a true artist. What a wonderful thing to be in life. If only more people could see the art, then a full circle would be had.

Later that night after several nightcaps near the fire were drunk Thomas went to the kitchen to bring Kristan an eggnog to sip on before bed. He brought it up to her room, knocked and set it on her nightstand. She was reading and said thank you. He left. Martin and Levi were still downstairs discussing paintings, hobbies, and past loves. Thomas walked the hallway. The lights on the vestibule lit up the paintings. He walked past all of them studying what he wasn't sure. But he felt compelled tonight to do that. He stopped at Martins Creole girlfriend from long ago. Martin met a lady in Louisiana and had a brief affair. He liked her but when he went to see her-she was gone. He painted her from a photograph. Maybe her name was on the photograph. Did Martin still have the photograph? Why was he dreaming up questions? Maybe it was the laugh. Oh brothers, go to bed, he told himself.

Breakfast came early the next morning and all came down to the breakfast table in the kitchen except Kristan. They all looked at one another.

"Do you think she had too much?" asked Levi.

"No, I didn't serve her but two drinks," Martin stated.

"Well, I did take her an eggnog to sip on up in bed." Thomas relented.

"Guys, she's a college girl now, most of them do shots of alcohol. Some puke, they live and learn." Levi explained.

"Except she's a freshman!" Martin became frazzled.

"She's had some drinks in high school. I've seen her at a Christmas party her junior year. She must have had three or four drinks back then. Oh goodness." Thomas recalled.

"Instead of us recoiling the past ways of youth I'll go check on her. I'm sure she is fine."

Levi ran upstairs to retrieve Kristan. After all today was the day on the mainland and they had to leave early. He knocked but no one came to the door. He opened it carefully to check. She wasn't in bed but over by the window. She had the window open and she was bent over a bowl from the stand.

"Kristan, you okay?" he asked.

"Levi, I'm fine. I woke up all hot, so I opened the window, and then when I sat down the room started spinning. Therefore, I grabbed this bowl just in case I lost it."

"Well, I'm no doctor but maybe you drank too much or you're getting the flu."

"I didn't drink too much. Two drinks is not too much over the holiday."

"Yeah, right. So it's the flu or a morning spell in the huge castle," he said and they both laughed.

"I'll be right down. I feel better already. Don't say anything, just that I overslept due to all my studying and tests."

"Sure thing." He left. She rose up and felt better, then got dressed. For one split second something else crossed her mind. Morning spell in the huge castle. Then she forgot about it.

The castle group took the boat to the mainland for shopping. Levi called his mom and wished her a Happy Thanksgiving, while Kristan shopped the drugstore and bought a personal item. Martin and Thomas walked about talking with locals wishing many a happy holiday. They picked up a few more items needed for the big dinner. The two of them loved, absolutely adored, cooking and caring for their niece. They decided that they needed to have the family down for more holidays now that Kristan was so close by at Vista University.

When they returned to the island, their private island, Thomas made some excuse about going to the stables to drop something off. He really wanted to look for that picture of the Creole girlfriend from long ago. He found it in a desk in the art studio. He didn't even want to look at the name. He didn't want to be wrong. He just knew in his heart a miracle was occurring. He stuffed it in his pocket. He said a quick prayer to his god that was always by his side, even the one he left back when he met Martin.

Chapter 13). Thanksgiving at the Uncles

Over coffee and kolaches Martin gave out the instructions for the day. Everyone would help, therefore, no one would exert themselves extensively and feel exhausted by days end. Rather stuffed, couch ready and maybe an aperitif with dessert in the evening. He had each person's instructions on a slip of paper with the whole menu placed atop his favorite French cookbook on a countertop stand next to a small wine stand.

"Looks delicious." Kristan read the menu.

"What time does the turkey go in?" asked Levi.

"Ten o'clock sharp," relayed Martin.

"What smells so good?" asked Kristan sitting down with her coffee.

"Thomas has made you one of his kolaches recipe. It is an old recipe made to go with beer. I think you'll like it. Sausage, cheddar cheese and jalapenos for a touch of spice. Actually a bit of bite," Martin said. "All in a biscuit. You can add some jam if you like or butter."

"Yes, please." Kristan thought it sounded delicious. "Where is the recipe from?"

Thomas walked in with a growler of beer, "It's an ancient recipe that I recently found in my mag 'Garden & Gun.'"

"I love trying new recipes."

"I promise I won't get you drunk but you must have a small glass of the beer I made with the biscuit-a perfect combo."

"If you say so."

The light banter in the breakfast room was heavenly.

Thomas had decided to not bring the past into the present until the day was over. He would wait until nightfall when everyone was satisfied, content, full or whatever. Then with the brandy being poured he would approach the love of his life besides God, of course, namely Martin. Martin was a man of the world, creative, truthful, hardworking, a gorgeous dark haired Frenchman if one ever saw one. Smooth and reliant he never disappointed, maybe only himself. But with his niece here Thomas could see how pleased he was, and her friend was certainly a human being that Martin loved to show him the how-tos in life: how to cook, how to prep fish, how to ride a horse, and possibly, how to drink a brandy. He didn't know if what he was dreaming could be real but it was worth a conversation. And that would be tonight. Thomas smiled. Maybe God had beautiful plans for this family.

Meanwhile after breakfast, before the cooking started, Martin took the pair to the stables for a quick lesson in riding. Neither of the two were scared of horses and the horses in the stable were a gentle lot. "Here's the equipment, Sheila will show you how to put it on and go with you around the place. Just follow her. See you when you get back. Enjoy."

Levi wore a dark green shirt and suitable brown plaid vest today with corduroys. He bought them when Kristan said her uncles owned the island. He speculated they might be rich and he wanted to shine, if only for the Thanksgiving celebration. He was glad the lady at the store asked him many questions. He felt like he fit in at this moment. Levi was having a great time.

Kristan had been on horses throughout her life, so this wasn't new. But she was not experienced or an excellent rider, just comfortable. She enjoyed the wind hitting her face, the animal succumbing to your whims and being out in nature. Rarely did she ever kick the abdomen, no need. She gave her beast a slight slap on the rump and off they went. Sheila took them on a trail, an eastern trail that went along the shoreline which faced Cumberland Island. When they slowed on purpose she pointed out the horses running free in a group across the water before them. What a beautiful majestic sight like something out of a novel from the dark ages!

"Incredible. I can hardly believe what I'm seeing." Levi pondered this moment. He was in awe.

"This is so worth it. Makes me happy America has wild horses, such a lovely site. It makes me feel like we respect the land and want to preserve it," Kristan felt proud and happy she was able to be here with her friend and revel in the glory of this place.

"I was hoping to see them on the trail. We have a few fields up ahead, run if you feel inclined and go steady with your horse. If not don't worry, use your skills to guide you. Running is vigorous and can use up your energy rather quickly. But give it a go for a short spell, you won't be disappointed," Sheila instructed. She felt confident they were both steady and poised riders by what she had seen so far. Running though was pure joy and quite courageous.

Upon returning to the stables Sheila took care of the horses after Levi and Kristan removed the saddles, bridles and bits. Sheila told them to go back to the house where Martin and Thomas were waiting to have them assist with the dinner. She was leaving the island shortly and would be off until next Monday. She and the gardener were off until Monday with the housekeeper and cook accompanying the family dinner at the table. Thomas and Martin kept four workers full time with holidays shared accordingly. It had worked out perfectly the last ten years. It was a family, anyone would tell you that.

Kristan changed clothes and put on a holiday dress she had purchased. Like Levi she wanted to impress and was thankful for the invitation to stay at this magnificent home.

All were assembled in the kitchen and followed their orders from Martin. Each person had three things to do and scurried around causing a little mayhem near the island. But after an hour and a half, all was done!

"See I told you it would go easy with all helping. Now we can sit back and relax," Martin said pleased with himself.

"No one ever sits back and relaxes on Thanksgiving. Do they?" asked Thomas.

"I'd like to take a picture of all of us cooks in the kitchen," Levi announced.

Levi raised his phone and snapped a picture of the four cooks in the kitchen.

"One more with my phone. Say cheese!" Kristan issued.

"See everyone in a few hours when we eat this delicious dinner."

Levi sent the picture to his mother via his phone then turned the TV on to watch some football. Kristan went outside by the pool to get better reception for her phone. Inside the house did not work very well.

"Mom, is it you?"

"Yes, honey. How are you? How's Thomas and Martin?"

"They are fantastic. I love them. They are being wonderful to us."

"Levi is enjoying himself, tremendously. Martin is showing him how to cook," Kristan said.

"Great. I miss you. Next year we will all be together. And I will see you at Christmas," Chloe reminded.

"Yes, I'll be home after finals around the tenth of December. I think I'm doing pretty well. I should make the Hope Scholarship."

"That is awesome. I hope you do. It will help with your loans to keep them low."

"Are you enjoying Paris? Has it changed at all?"

"Of course, it has. But my memories are still there and we have visited some of the same places. It's so beautiful and nostalgic. Very romantic place. You should come sometime, maybe when you are done with school."

"Someday, I will."

About thirty minutes before the meal 'extravaganza' Thomas poured everyone a beer from his brew and they went around the castle looking at all the Christmas trees. There was around seven or so large trees with mini ones in the bedrooms. Levi wanted a picture of Kristan in front of the big tree next to the fireplace in the great room.

"Kristan, stand there. Let me take a picture. I love that tree."

"Let me see how it turned out, and the one with us cooks in the kitchen."

"Here it is. Hey, wait, it hasn't sent to my mother yet," said Levi.

"You have to go out by the pool to get better reception."

"Oh, and guess what? I'm out of power. Let me go charge it." Levi ran up to his room to charge his phone. When he returned it was time for dinner.

The two servants joined the four chefs which made for six attendees at the table set for a King and Queen with their special guests. Thomas had overdone the table settings and one just had to guess at which utensil to use and when to use it. Plates galore, double napkins, three stems and bouquets of dried flowers with recently alive items from the swamp (marshes) and surrounding areas. Happy Thanksgiving and Joyous Noel to be sure. What was that music playing Levi wondered?

"A toast to our guests and extended family," Thomas made the first toast.

"Cheers."

"Cheers, if anyone is wondering what is playing it is the music box channel I found. They play these songs of Christmas off a tin record that you have to wind up. It's delightful don't you think?" Thomas told the group. Levi nodded his head in approval. Thomas seemed to know what he was thinking at times.

The servants finished cleaning up the dinner mess after everyone chipped in to help. Dessert would come later with an aperitif of brandy by the fire. Kristan went into the study to take a nap and Levi followed by retrieving his phone from the charger. He resent the photo to his mother in Baton Rouge, who was really in Texas visiting her sister, then texted a couple of classmates he'd met this semester and one from The Bean Dip where he worked wishing them all a Happy Thanksgiving. He didn't tell any of them where he was. Actually, he couldn't believe where he was himself. Dreamy is how it felt. He laid down for a quick nap himself before the fireside brandy and dessert.

Meanwhile the uncles gathered in a downstairs bar or game room. Thomas said he wanted to talk with Martin about something important. He had no clue what was about to be said. Thomas had changed his mind on waiting for the brandy and would do it now. This would allow time to sink in and then no arguments before bed.

When Levi awoke his phone had exploded in texts. But he couldn't read them. His phone had charged but now he needed to go to the pool to see what they said. So he did.

Thomas said, "I have something to show you. I'm not sure of anything but my heart and my god tell me it may be something."

"Do go on. I'm intrigued," said Martin. He envisioned that Thomas wanted to go on some international cruise through the Mediterranean near Greece.

Thomas pulled out a picture and gave it to Martin.

"A picture of one of my gals I painted. No need to be jealous. I told you everything there is to know." He returned the picture to Thomas.

Levi sat on one of the pool lounge chairs and began reading the text messages. There was a few from his new friends telling him to send pictures and one from a girl he'd met at The Bean Dip. Then he saw there was three from his mother. One said Happy Thanksgiving. Another was a picture of his two younger siblings. The third read like this...

"I don't mean to startle you but the picture of the cooks in the kitchen has me curious. One of the men looks familiar. I may know him from a long time ago." Levi read this and didn't think too much about it. Maybe he should ask the uncles himself. He sat out by the pool which was all lit up thinking about this.

Thomas said, "Come let's really look at that picture in the hallway before we have our brandy and pie." They walked upstairs towards the paintings of Martins ex-girlfriends.

Levi found himself walking up the stairs to go and view the painting. Maybe he had been drawn to it because it did look like someone he knew. It looked like his mother. Thomas had said the paintings were ex-girlfriends of Martin.

The two were so involved looking at her they didn't notice Levi.

"What's her name?"

"Oh Levi. Yes. Her name?" Thomas etched out.

"What is her name?" He pointed to the dark brown haired beauty on the wall.

"Her name is Clementine. Clementine," he said a second time.

"Martin, that is my mother's name."

"Your mother's name?" Martin questioned.

"It's a creole name from way back. We call her Tina." Levi explained.

"There are not too many Clementine's in this world." Thomas added.

"No there are not." Levi stated.

"Where are you from?" Martin could hardly speak now. He asked almost as a side note trying not to show his weakened voice.

"Baton Rouge, Louisiana, sir," said Levi, calmly.

"Baton Rouge?" Martin asked rather slowly.

"I believe we should go downstairs, pour a brandy and eat some pumpkin pie," said Thomas quietly and directly.

The music box station was still playing tunes as they all entered the great room with an enormous fireplace. Things were in limbo, settling in, but what was settling in? The unknown.

Chapter 14). The Unknown

Silence came over them while Kristan joined the group fireside. The servants, guests tonight, served them pie and Thomas poured the brandy for all. The music box station played softer tunes of Christmas while everyone enjoyed their pumpkin pie made by Kristan.

"It's very good my dear. You did wonderful," said Martin.

"All you chefs did a marvelous job today. I think this is the best Thanksgiving I've ever had," said Kristan.

"My thoughts exactly. This day has been a memorable one to be sure," said Levi.

"We continue to count our blessings as they roll in. I think," Martin issued.

"Martin, pardon me, but do you know this woman in this photo?" Levi showed Martin a picture of his mother from his phone.

"Yes, I did know her but haven't seen her in many years. I don't know if there is anything here to discuss further until ..."

"Until we ask my mother," added Levi.

"Will it shock her?" Thomas questioned. "And should we ask her?"

"What on earth are y'all talking about?" asked Kristan.

"Kristan, remember the painting upstairs?" Levi asked her.

"There are so many. Which one?" she asked.

Thomas pulled out the picture to show her, then turned it over to reveal the name. "It says Clementine."

"Clementine. One of your girlfriends you painted?" Kristan asked, still unknowing of the situation at hand.

"Kristan, my mother's name is Clementine," Levi said.

She looked between them, back and forth, with a puzzled look on her face.

"I'm ready for a brandy," she said. "Tell me what is up?"

Thomas handed her a brandy.

"My dear it might be possible, a long shot I'd say, that Levi's mother and I, as we did date way back when, that maybe, it's possible, Levi could be my son."

"Then you must ask your mother. It's possible you're not you know." Kristan directed her thoughts to Levi about the truth.

"I know. But, wow, maybe it's true. You do look like the lady in the painting," Thomas added.

"Tonight, I think we should just linger on possibilities. I'll ask her tomorrow as she is not at home and out to her sister's house." Levi made a plan.

"Tonight, Levi, you are out on the ocean, and endless possibilities exist there in the deep, deep blue." Kristan stated like a dream on the horizon.

"Well put, my dear," Martin.

A few jokes were told, while Thomas noted the deep never ending laughs, that seemed to tie the room together. How rich is life that possibilities and unknowns bring one another together, by chance encounter or mere directions in life?

Friday morning came early but Levi and Kristan set out to go exploring the waterways in the boat. They assured the uncles they wouldn't go too far. Turkey sandwiches were made and packed with coffee to go. They were off and on their way to another adventure. This place was a prize and both Levi and Kristan set about having another great day.

It was a calm morning with no waves or movement and slightly chilly. The boat maneuvered skillfully mostly all on its own. They glided past the Island of horses out to sea where the ocean was endless. Few boats were out this early, save for a fisherman or two. Levi spotted a couple of dolphins, he slowed and they both watched the dolphins delight in their ocean familiarity offering a show. Once they sped up and went perpendicular to the shore the dolphins played again in their wake. Nature surprises the eyes that watch its beauty. From this area the horses were galloping along the shore in a group splashing the water with their momentum and enormous weight. Levi turned the wheel over to Kristan to take them back. Once around the curve she slowed and they ate turkey sandwiches. Life can be blissful at times and this was one of those times.

She was thinking how nice it was she brought, Levi, her new friend to the island, never thinking that it could become something as profound in his life with the announcement made last night. He was smiling, maybe he was thinking the same thing. Maybe he would find out today if Martin was his father he never knew about. Maybe she would perform that test kit she bought on the mainland and get that idea out of her head. As soon as she got back to the castle she had to do it. She would. She hadn't told anyone her thoughts.

Upon returning she ran up the stairs while Levi headed for the pool area to call his mother. Kristan retrieved the test kit and made haste for the bathroom she shared with Levi. Once she did it she walked with the strip to the window upstairs that overlooked the pool area and saw Levi. He was talking with his mother. It was likely morning in Baton Rouge or Texas she thought. He was pacing. Was he scared to ask her something so personal? But he was involved and they had a good relationship. Kristan felt like she would be honest with him. She kept watching for a sign. Waiting. Wondering. What was next? She didn't know. She saw him smile. That had to be good. She looked at her test strip in her hand.

"Kristan dear, is everything okay?" Thomas asked her.

She looked again at the strip. Positive. What? She looked at Thomas and back at the test strip. "I don't know. I don't know."

Thomas surmised but instead of asking, he held her for a short while.

"I think I'm pregnant."

"Do you know who the father is?"

"It's not Levi. We are friends. Please don't tell anyone until I figure this out."

"Your secret is safe. I'm here if you need an ear."

"Thank you. Oh my. I have to tell my mother. I'll tell her in a couple weeks at Christmas."

The Thanksgiving holiday ended on Saturday when the two departed the island after thanking her uncles for a wonderful time. Levi and Martin discussed the prospect that was verified to be true from his mother, about this welcome though unexpected news. It actually meant in some way Kristan and Levi were cousins with her mother and his father as brother and sister. Martin and Levy embraced in a hug and promised to talk and see each other again after it all sunk in. Talk about a long shot coincidence. Kristan decided to not tell anyone about being pregnant, as yet, before her mother. Thomas promised to keep the secret if she did tell her mother. She promised.

A week and a half of classes and exams consumed them upon return to Vista University. How exciting that one semester was finished. But on the other hand of that happiness existed a big fear of what to do now. She knew who the father was but the issue was hers and hers alone. She let that sink in. Instead of fear she took with her the realm that she would be in control and make this decision on her own. What to do? Not exactly perfect timing. A baby with a father she had broken up with who was excited to start his life in the air force. He was just waiting to get in. She had just started her college life and now she was pregnant by Thanksgiving. She scolded herself. One night after exams she wrote it all down on paper and made a plan of all the options. What would be best for everyone involved? There were three lives in this picture and she controlled two of them. Kristan decided that two was greater than one so it was up to her. That was simplistic but so what. Whatever you believed in it was her decision. She told herself God made us women and we must be strong. He would guide her but she was in charge. And that rested her mind for the time being. She smiled. She would find a plan that worked.

She called her mom. She said she was excited for Christmas and she would see her in a week. One more English class with Professor Knox before finals. Probably the last poem reading. She recalled.

One of the poems about kids... 1st was death, 2nd was oceans and 3rd is a kid poem...

After class Kristan asked the reader if she could write the poem out for her. She wanted to keep it for good luck.

Perfect Package

Said bond truly latches like no other.

Amazing firsts like building a pyramid.

Multiple milestones bigger and better,

Lovely cherubs sending arrows of

Sweetness directly into my heart.

Soft clouds freshly scent into my arms.

Nature's purity and pitched songs,

Make me dance and follow her tune.

Immediate for many and some struck in stages.

The coo draws the hesitant admirer,

Like burped relief, clean bottoms and silent afternoons.

Helpless and growing all in my hands.

This perfect package a lullaby in my arms,

Nothing more fine, existence is mine.

Chapter 15). Christmas at Home

Kristan didn't have much time to think about her predicament until she hit the road to drive home for Christmas. Reality set in and she became a bit stressed thinking about it. She would tell her mother and together they would formulate a plan. Would she stay at school with a growing belly? People would look at her and know. What would she tell them? She's married. No. despite feeling strong about what she intended to do other people's faces and opinions would enter into the situation. It was a big deal. Her mother would know what to do. Moms know everything. First she would say, "Honey, you should have prepared."

Pulling up the driveway in the late afternoon she could see the decorations placed outside all lit up, and once inside she saw the tree was decorated and lit and the house smelled good. It was good to be home. She brought her suitcase and other bags up to her room and laid upon her bed. Mom and Dad must be out. She rested and prepared herself. She would tell her tonight. She couldn't waste another minute. Her Instagram was popping up with notifications from high school friends with pics of Christmas trees and get-togethers. She looked forward to seeing a few people. But not Noah. How could she hide this secret? Best not to get together. She would stay busy with family, shopping and watching Christmas movies, maybe even doing some baking with her mom while her dad was at work.

There was a knock at her door. It was her mother. "Come in."

"Hi dear, welcome home!" She got up and hugged her mother.

"Thanks. I'm glad to be here."

"Dad has a business meeting tonight, so it's you and me."

"Good. We can catch up and I'll tell you all about Thanksgiving with the uncles."

"Perfect. Would you like to go to the Mexican restaurant or my favorite Italian?'

"Let's do Mexican at the plaza near the place where they sell the Xmas trees."

"Okay. How about in an hour?"

"I'll be ready then." This gave Kristan some time to prepare her words.

Sitting in a booth munching on chips and salsa contemplating what to order Chloe asked her, "Everything okay? You look preoccupied."

"I do?"

"Yes. You do."

"Well, I do have something to tell you but it's not about school."

Kristan reached for her phone and pulled up her Instagram account, scrolled to a fellow student that she really didn't know who didn't go to college and showed her mother the picture.

"Someone had a baby? Cute baby. Mother looks young. Do you know her?"

"No, not really. Someone from our class last year that dropped out of school to have a baby. She lives with her mother and they are raising the baby."

"That is a difficult thing to do, not graduate, have a baby, and then raise it. It's a full time job. I feel sorry for her. A baby is 24/7, a selfless act of love. Still very hard."

"I know. Well, I don't really know but everyone says it's hard to do."

"The father may know or not and the work ends up on the mother for a lifetime. Not to mention the cost which is immense."

Kristan closed her phone and set it back down.

The waitress came and took their order. Then left.

"So what do you have to tell me?"

"I'm pregnant. At least the test kit was positive."

Her mother's eyes never left Kristan's face. Kristan had to look down and away. She studied her taking it in but not really. Disbelief.

"Seriously?"

"Uh, yes."

"Wow. I wasn't expecting that news."

"Neither was I."

Her mother reached for her hand and held it. She conveyed that everything was going to be all right. Her mother swallowed and drank her drink. Trying to think of her next words there was a moment of silence.

"Do you have a plan?"

"I think I do. I need your help."

"We must tell your dad and the father."

"Dad, yes. The father, no, for now. I'll tell him later."

The food was served and they ate in silence. When they got home her mother gave her a big hug and said, "Meet me in the office and we'll discuss this some more."

The pair talked for an hour and came up with a plan. Chloe decided on the way home that this would be her daughter and her life, her ideas. It had to be. She knew that what she wanted and how she would handle it might be two different ideas. This was her life. She would guide her, not tell her what to do. Oh my. This was huge but solvable and to think that a little life now lived inside her daughter. At least it didn't happen in high school. Thank goodness for that. Chloe told her that she would tell her father so he had some time to digest it. Fathers needed a little more time for this delicate news. She was sure of that.

And so by the third day home the news was broke and everyone, all three of them, were informed. Instead of drama there was peace. To be sure one could change their mind with such a grand thing as a baby but for now the plan was hatched.

Chloe warmed up to the plan that Kristan had. Though, it wouldn't have been her plan, she admired her for her bravery, her willingness and forethought not to mention it was morally right in the eyes of God and the church. Christmas was going to be much more this year. Her and Kristan baked cookies and took them to a few nursing homes in the area. They wrapped presents for those in need and took them to her church. They attended midnight mass as they had done for years. It was good to have her home. A few of her friends came over and sat by the fire, roasting marshmallows, eating cookies, and told stories of the first semester at college. Kristan avoided any talk of Noah, saying it was over, even spilling a few secrets of parties at Vista. She did hint that she might take a semester off to work and save some money doing a couple classes online. She blamed it on trying to get into nursing school, which everybody knew was next to impossible. There just weren't enough slots. You had to have straight A's and take these impossible tests. No one could understand why it was so difficult. You weren't a doctor or physician assistant. They kept nurses from doing more, more that they were capable of, especially the intensive care nurses who could run a code better than an ER doctor. Maybe nurses were just handmaidens like the days of yesterday used to call them. Doctors ran the show-that was for certain. Would it ever change? Nurse friends of Chloe's complained to her and suggested she not do nursing. This gave her pause. Maybe God would intervene.

Between Christmas and New Year's Eve Kristan and her parents drove to Savannah and set her up in an apartment with three other girls. This would be a temporary place until fall semester. This is how her plan would work.

And just like that after a few phone calls a whole new temporary life was set up. All this trouble for six months or so because she made an error. She touched her stomach, not an error, baby, you are a home run! She didn't know if it was her faith or religion, her mother, maybe even her uncles but something made Kristan feel important, that she had a mission to complete. She prayed and everything seemed to be falling in place. Just. Like. That. Her mother had a friend that ran an apartment complex and set her up with a couple other roommates in school down in Savannah. She would live there and take two classes online from Vista, maybe work downtown if she desired. The Ghost Tours were hiring. She could work there part time and rest as much as she needed. Time would fly. She'd miss her mom but it was just until fall semester or whenever the baby came into the world. Her parents helped her unpack and settle in. She would not have a car this semester but everything seemed to be in walking distance and her mother's friend had a flexible schedule to help her when she needed it.

"This is Madison, or is it Victoria?" Chloe's friend initiated.

"I'm Madison, Victoria is my twin." An athletic looking and tall black girl stood up from the couch to greet Kristan. Kristan smiled and introduced herself.

"Victoria lives here, too. She's not back from holiday break. She went skiing in Colorado." Madison further instructed.

"Do y'all look alike?" Kristan asked the obvious question when talking about twins.

"We do."

"I guess I have six months to learn the difference," she said with a light laugh.

Another girl walked in and looked surprised to see everyone in the living room.

"Pearl, we have a new roommate. This is Kristan."

Pearl looked at Kristan. She studied her for a moment, maybe to figure out this stranger and why she was here. Kristan stared at her for a moment too long maybe.

Something she couldn't put her finger on.

"Hi, I'm Kristan. Looking forward to being here with y'all."

"If ya like I'm going out with some friends tonight for pizza. You can join me."

"Sure. What time?"

"Seven. I'm driving. Meet you in the parking lot."

Kristan walked her parents to their car, said goodbye, and knew it would be a half year or so before she saw them again. Hugs and 'I love you's' were exchanged. But what wasn't spoken was words of I'm sorry.

"Thank you for letting me make this right. You are the best parents a girl could have."

And like that her new life, albeit temporary, began.

Pearl drove them to the restaurant Vinnie Van Go Go's and they ordered after sitting down at a table. The two chatted on and on until the reveal.

"I knew there was something about you when I walked into the apartment," Pearl exclaimed.

"I also knew something was amiss about you," Kristan threw back at her.

"What? How could you tell? I'm not that far along, at all. I'm still figuring it out. No one knows." Pearl explained.

"Okay, your secrets safe with me," Kristan needed a friend right now and Pearl would do just fine. Pearl was pale with porcelain skin and thin features. She had long flowing reddish brown hair with lots of body. She exposed a lone tattoo on her inner arm. It was a rose with color, very pretty, thought Kristan.

"I think I'm going to work at the ghost tours. Good idea?" Kristan asked.

"Great idea. Lots of fun. Most of them are at night but one is during the day. That one might just be the spookiest, ya know?" Pearl talked on and on.

"Then that's one I'll apply for. Maybe being scared will detour my mind from myself."

Pearl studied her new friend some more. The two both had their minds made up and couldn't be further from each other. Pearl contemplated Kristan's extraordinary challenge and sacrifice set before her.

"What?" asked Kristan.

"Better you than me," said Pearl. These two were like dear old friends after 45 minutes. At least they had each other. Kristan's phone buzzed. She picked it up and it was Jeremy.

Facetime call. "Jeremy!"

"Kristan, hey! I heard you weren't coming back until next semester."

"Yes. Oh I miss you so much!"

"I have a car this semester. Can I come visit some weekend?"

"Sure. Wait let me ask her."

She put the camera on Pearl.

"Hi, I'm Jeremy."

"Hi. I'm Pearl, Kristan's new friend."

"Can I come visit my dear friend from English class?"

"Yes. Come next weekend. We have a sleeper sofa."

"Okay, it's set. See you next weekend. I'll send the address. It's very easy to find and its downtown with so much to do."

"Kristan, you sound wonderful. Can't wait."

"Bye Jeremy!"

The Facetime call ended.

"He's such a sweetie."

"Can't wait to meet him."

Kristan and Pearl returned back to the apartment and both went to their rooms. Kristan applied online to work part time at a ghost tour company. And Pearl made a doctor's appointment.

Chapter 16). High School Swim Meet

Victoria and Madison were both competitive high school swimmers. They stood out as the only black swimmers from their area. And they were good but not good enough to secure a scholarship on a college team in Division A. A couple schools came calling but the tuition was 40K and the scholarship 10K. Their parents could not afford to send them out of state on this scenario. They just missed the team in Alabama at a great little college out in the country by mere slivers or fractions of a second on times. Most of the time their parents had conversations and complained about football having enormous amounts of money and other sports suffering with nothing to offer smart girls with an incredible talent. When would colleges wake up and decide other sports were important to display some love to? A swim meet could have a band, food, and a more celebratory atmosphere. Besides more people could do swimming than play football. The discussion was endless and usually ended with that's the way it is. Football brings in the money so therefore it's theirs. What if no one came to watch? No concessions? Empty stadiums. Never in a million years did anyone think like that. Still their mother tried and tried but her hands were tied. To deaf ears. She felt it in her heart so she knew the good Lord planted that seed. She just had to find a way.

"Our sister is swimming in Savannah this weekend, come with us to watch. It's very exciting ladies. They serve food and lots of eye candy!" She said that to get their obvious non attentive appeal.

"Eye candy? At a swim meet?"

"Gotcha!"

"Seriously, what's up?" Kristan questioned.

"Oh, there are lots of great bodies walking around."

"But they're like sophomores in high school-no thanks."

"Guys, the older siblings who are college guys come too," Victoria explained.

"Okay, I'm in. I need to check out the men from Savannah for future reference."

Pearl looked at Kristan. She knew she was placating Victoria and had no plans to scope out any visions of the future. "Sure ladies, I'm game."

"Plus we can cheer for our sister-maybe she'll rock faster times and get a real scholarship to Auburn. She wants it I know," Madison told the story. They could all cheer her on. "Besides my mom will be there and she'll pay for everything. It's her last child, her last hope."

Pearl and Kristan sat higher up in the bleachers but close enough to Madison and Victoria's family. They followed the program and circled her name plus a couple other names Kristan knew from her county. The venue was awesome-it had a scoreboard that lit up the names of the swimmers, unlike most areas with just a lane marker. The two tried to educate themselves on strokes, times and heats as fast as they could. Victoria and Madison's mother bought them chicken sandwiches, chips and drinks. When the student swimmer was up, all were standing to cheer her on. One didn't suspect under water any swimmer could hear the crowd. Pearl would have to ask that question if she could remember it later on. The swimming pool area became very loud with buzzers, whistles, slapping of the water, and crowds yelling. In between some music played and it echoed in the area loudly.

For a moment Pearl became bored and she looked at an odd man about six rows down. Why did he look out of place? She studied him some more. Well, he looks to be about almost a grandpa in age, non-American by country origin, and he was reading the newspaper upside down. Peculiar for sure. So she looked away and followed something else but she was drawn back to him and wondered which child he was cheering for. She waited and looked for a child to come up to him asking how she or he did. But none came. How odd. If she had binoculars then by all means she would have looked at the newspaper to see if it was English. But by the headline she knew it was not. Her gut instinct told her this was extremely odd and it bothered her but she declined to tell Kristan because she did not want to disturb her new friend who was in a motherly way as well. Definitely, she would not upset her in any way. This small moment made Pearl feel watched, paranoid, and disturbed and if anyone knew Pearl she was not those things. The man turned around several times and looked but not at her just around her. Creepy. Geez. This is a swim meet get over it she told herself!

Their sister was up swimming in the 100 breast stroke; they all stood and clapped and yelled. They could follow her twenty-five yards at a time. Each turn put a new time up and held her position. The first twenty-five she went fast but steady and didn't worry about anyone ahead or behind. She looked strong and beautiful in the water. She had graceful strokes that flowed over the water like a dolphin or mermaid. The second twenty-five she was behind, yet still steady. Victoria looked up at Kristan and Pearl and had her fingers locked in luck, she yelled, "keep watching!"

Somewhere, wherever magic or talent exists, she upped the ante and began to stroke faster, harder and you could see she had vision to excel. Her split was now going to be faster than the first fifty. How exciting!!

Madison was so taken by her little sister she began to cry. The third twenty-five was the fastest and she was now ahead and going faster. She was ahead by more than a body length. Her competitors were long gone behind her. Fantastic. Kristan and Pearl didn't know times but she came in first and looked so pleased. Out of the pool she came once everyone was finished. Her name had a 1st place next to it. She beamed a broad smile up to her parents and siblings in the stands.

"Hey, maybe that'll get her a scholarship," Kristan said to Victoria.

"That and a few more like it will," she replied.

Kristan was happy for this break of going to a swim meet. She had swum in summer meets at the local pool therefore she understood the times and strokes and could help Pearl. A two hour break was at hand until finals tonight at six. They headed outside for fresh air and to walk around. Pearl looked around for the mysterious man but he was nowhere to be found. Mystery man disappeared. Maybe she was seeing things. No she told herself. It was real. But she forgot about it. For now. Pearl glanced at Kristan's stomach, she wasn't showing, and neither was she. Her doctor's appointment was this coming week. She had no hesitation. She just hadn't told anyone of her plans. Her decision was made. She felt fine about it. She just didn't want to talk about it to anyone. Not even to her new friend. She told her a lie. It was best. She would talk about it afterwards. Pearl had no family. Her mother and father were dead and she wasn't about to start one right now. This was a mistake she would take care of. That is how she looked at it. Though, she thought her new friend very brave. Pearl didn't have that courage or friends that cared about her. No one cared about her and wouldn't care about a baby. The father doesn't even know. It was someone at a party who never called. Next weekend it would be over. She smiled. One more week to think about it. Then all is done.

Finals were even more fun than that afternoon. Their sister was in first place in two events and second in the other two. The music played loud and was apparently her choice when she was the first place qualifier. She looked on fire during those moments. Intensity hung over the crowd which was less this evening with everyone there having an athlete in the finals. The sister knew every tenth counted. The electronic counters were amazing. One could even see how fast off the block an athlete went, which helped in a small way. The younger sister placed first in each event, 100 breaststroke and 100 backstroke, and received second in the 100 free and 100 butterfly. Amazing. She was amazing, an all-around swimmer good in all strokes. Her family was extremely proud of her and invited everyone to dinner downtown Savannah after the event.

The family received a call from a coach who was very pleased. They would talk next week about her future plans. All in all it didn't get much better than this. The twins decided they would be going to different cities to watch her swim in the coming year. If it hadn't happened for them then they would pour their love and devotion unto her. It couldn't have happened to a better girl they thought. And seeing their momma so pleased, it brought them much happiness, too.

A large table in back at the brewery held the party that night and everyone seemed so joyous. A few other parents came and a couple of toasts were made. Moon River Brewing on 21 W Bay Street was near the river and centrally located. The college students thought too bad we can't use our fake ID's to get a beer but they'd come back here for sure. It wasn't one of those hangouts anyway for under age college students. Those were off the main drag so to speak. Kristan and Pearl weren't drinking anyway these days.

Moon burgers and hot crab meat dip were perfect and Kristan ate every bite. The two headed for their car about three blocks away. Pearl was driving as Kristan didn't have a car this semester. Once in the car Pearl noticed a jacked up big black truck, which roared its engine and pulled out fast in front of them, then stopped blocking their exit. One couldn't even see in the windows. It revved its engine some more right in front of them then squealed away. What in tarnation was that all about thought Pearl? One more thing was all she could think of. Never mind that dudes do that all the time to impress or show off. Or intimidate. The girls looked at each other and Pearl locked the doors to be safe.

Chapter 17). Pearl's Doctor's Appointment

Pearl left the apartment early for her doctor's appointment. She didn't tell anyone about what kind of doctor she was seeing. In fact, Kristan was the only roommate that knew she was pregnant. She was okay with that because later she would tell her she terminated it because, well, she wasn't her. She couldn't do it. She wasn't altruistic like Kristan. She had no parents anymore, so who really would care, one way or the other. She wasn't allowed to eat or drink and needed an empty stomach because she would require anesthesia. She was past the seven weeks where she could have taken the RU 486 pill, or European pill. How easy would that have been? She just didn't know for a while as her periods were not regular and with her recent move she put it out of her mind. She was too late.

The doctor's office told her she would be fine, they do this all the time. She took an Uber to the office because she wouldn't be able to drive. She lied about someone picking her up. She would stay the maximum time and then Uber home. Perfect. All worked out, the plan was in motion. Everyone was very nice at the clinic. They informed her and seemed genuine. She pondered what her mother might think about this. Would she care? She might. But Pearl was young and the time was wrong, or was it? On with it. Her mind was made up.

The surgery went smooth. Pearl was ten weeks. She didn't want to know if it was a girl or a boy. It was an it. She slept a long time, then they gave her some liquids and asked about the pain or cramping. They gave her some medicine in the IV for pain and waited awhile longer. The bleeding was minimal but it could be more in the next twenty four hours. She sat up in the chair and used the restroom. Later on they told her she could go when her ride returned. She pulled all her papers together, walked around and felt ready to leave. She called her an Uber and slipped out when it arrived. A couple miles and she would be home. She tipped the Uber and told him to wait five minutes until she got in the door. He seemed to understand and waited five minutes. Once inside she made haste for her room, locked it and stretched out on the bed. She already had her drinks by the bedside and soft foods. She'd planned this out so she could do it by herself. No more worries for her. She fell asleep.

She woke early the next day and left the apartment early again. She went out and bought some new clothes, more stylish, then made a surprise visit to the big church in town. She pulled into the parking lot, parked and walked to the front doors. She hadn't been here since her parents died three years earlier. The door was open and she walked a few rows in and sat down. Likely God would say she was too late. Sinner. She figured she still loved God, so he must still love her and that's how she began her prayer. The prayers always felt a hundred times more holy when said in a church. Her next prayer was for Kristan to keep her safe during her pregnancy and a tiny little prayer for the baby. It would be a baby sent to parents who would love her, from the sacrifice of a beautiful young girl who was brave enough to do the right thing. Pearl felt better knowing God would be pleased she was praying for someone else. That was a kind thing to do. She felt God's blessing and walked out of the church.

She went to the grocery store and picked up a few things for Kristan and herself. She would look after Kristan now. She felt it her duty. Eventually she would tell her the truth. This coming weekend, though, her friend from Vista University would be visiting. They would take him on a tour of the city. There was so much to do in Savannah, one would never tire of the old houses, the gardens, the restaurants and bars, the riverboat excursions, sightseeing, not to mention the ghost tours. And how about just plain walking around, window shopping and eating salt water taffy.

"Hey Pearl, where you been? Haven't seen you in two or three days," Kristan asked.

"Sweetie, I've been taking it easy, getting ready to hit the town with your friend when he arrives," Pearl was a real sweetie herself.

"Yes, Jeremy comes this weekend for a few days. We could let him sleep on the sofa or you and I could sleep together and give him my room. What do ya think?"

"I like that idea. You and me and a slumber party." Pearl meant what she said. Kristan shook her head in the yes motion warming to her own idea.

"I wouldn't mind having a warm body and someone to talk with when the moon rises outside my window. It might help to talk with someone while this baby grows, you too." Kristan went on and on.

"Yeah, okay. I bought some groceries for the weekend. It will be nice to have a guy around here. He's cute too." Pearl went and put the groceries away, then closed the door and took a nap.

Later on the two gathered in the family room and went through the TV channels looking for a movie. They couldn't find one. They turned the TV off and chatted some.

"You know after the baby comes I'm going to travel during my time off from college. I guess I'll need to earn some money to do that," Kristan talked out loud about future plans.

"I think there's an app or emails you can receive to get discount rates on flights and such," Pearl said.

"Let me look that up. I'll google it."

"Certain airlines have great rates. I'm not sure how to get low hotel rates but air B n B rates can be seriously low," Pearl added.

"Where should I go?" Kristan questioned.

"Where would you like to go? Or where have you not been?" Pearl played along.

"Hawaii, Mexico, Canada, west coast, mountains ..." Kristan named off some countries.

"Vegas," Pearl said.

"Vegas?" Kristan questioned. "Vegas, hey, I like that."

"My mom used to go to Vegas and raved about it. The lights, the hotels, the casinos and all that clanking of coins, plus the entertainment can be fabulous."

"Sounds like fun," Kristan said.

"One time she said she was out there in around 2012 or so and she thought someone was following her," Pearl recalled.

"Following her? Like a stalker?"

"Yes, she went to a club bar in a hotel and she thought someone was following her-then in the nightclub a guy ran into her real hard which almost made her fall over. He kept going didn't say sorry or ask if she was all right. Later, the next day, a guy at breakfast kept staring at her wearing a San Francisco baseball shirt. Said she couldn't shake it. She wondered what on earth a lady like her could have done. She was scared to death and never went back to Vegas."

"Did you believe her?" Kristan asked.

"Yes, I did. Her brother had been in trouble with the law and never caught a break. They pounced on him over and over. He ended up with a long rap sheet of basically nothing. They hated him and wanted him to stay away but he kept suing them in court. He was a pest to them. Anyway, I'm not sure if someone was directed to scare my mother but you should have seen the look on her face. The blood drained out of it just talking about it. I saw her shaking when she talked about it. My mom was a good lady always tried to do the right thing in life. My brother ended up serving five years in prison for a threatening email; my mom thought whomever kept threatening her aught be in for five years."

"Thanks for sharing that Pearl. I'm sorry your family is gone now. But we are becoming friends-so that's a good thing. Did they ever leave her alone?"

"She finally found out that from a surgery she had the feds were able to track her from an established network of domestic and global surveillance system by way of state and public health departments under WHO. But first she went crazy from the bombardment online and in person. Her brother is still alive but I don't see him. He never did find justice. Kind of a big brother thingy. You'll never win. Stay out of trouble and don't piss anyone off. But hey, who can do that. Isn't this a free country with rights?"

"Oh Pearl, you should run for office where your voice can be heard-loud and clear!"

"You think? I do like the little people. And if you do it then its fair game I reckon. On another note I'm looking forward to your friend visiting."

"What's his name again?"

"Jeremy, and he loves literature."

"Literature?"

"Yes. Romeo and Juliet literature."

"He's a Romeo. Oh good! Can't wait."

Chapter 18). Jeremy Visits Savannah

"Jeremy, come in, come in!" Kristan was excited to see her friend and English class cohort right here in Savannah.

In walked Jeremy, tall, young and smiling. Pearl checked him out. Even cuter in person and look at that smile. He's a woman pleaser. His hair had slight curls, dark brown and his eyes were chocolates. Pearl stood up to greet him, welcoming him to their place.

"Hello, I'm Jeremy." He took her hand and kissed the top of it. Pearl's eyes fell to the floor. He took note of her sincerity in his action, which made his personality even warmer.

"I'm Pearl." Pearl was lean with beautiful soft skin yet her words came out strong. She just seemed like the kind of person you'd like to go out with and listen to her stories. One just got the sense she was part gypsy in nature-maybe it was her green eyes. They seemed sort of musical. Jeremy was a bit taken and lingered there taking it in.

"You two should definitely sit down for a while and chat, learn about each other. I'll put your suitcase in Pearl's room-we are giving you a room so you don't have to sleep on the couch," remarked Kristan.

Pearl went to get drinks while Jeremy sat on the sofa and relaxed taking in the apartment. Pearl joined him and Kristan went to stand and look out the window. She saw a tow truck removing a car. That car parks there every day.

She wondered why they were taking it away now after parking there every day since she'd come to town.

"Why do you think they are towing that car, Pearl? The red one out front."

"Are they? That's funny, it's been parked there every day for months during the day but not at night."

"Seems strange."

"My mother used to say every time they towed a car for no reason somebody wanted you bugged," Pearl said. Kristan turned around and looked at her.

"Seriously?"

"Huh?" asked Jeremy.

"She should know her mother had a brother in the federal pen," answered Kristan.

Everyone looked at her. Staring.

"Oh, I'm sorry I don't mean to scare you. It was not serious, he didn't rape, murder or steal, didn't plant a bomb. Hell, he didn't even lie, he just wanted to prove his case in court and they prevented him from doing so. He kept pursuing it year after year. Not sure what they wanted with my mother, maybe to scare her away. I heard a senator say once they have six ways to Sunday to get you. I guess my mom was the seventh way."

"Oh Pearl, it's just we don't hear about people in prison every day. We are not scared or mistrusting of you."

"Good. I'm vulnerable but I've led a good life and plan to forever. However long that is." Pearl meant every word but she was known to find herself in predicaments that were not thought out in advance. Her personality led her to experiment and be more trustworthy.

Kristan looked back out at the car getting towed. "My mother had her car towed twice, the blue one back in 2012 in Atlanta and the white one this past December 2020 in Florida of all places. Do you suppose someone is trying to get her? And for what?" After a pause they all laughed. But this thought would stay with Kristan for a long time.

"You'd like to think that you are the only one listening to your voice singing loudly in the car, or maybe cursing someone out who is not in the car, or better yet, when you think you are alone with your thoughts expressing them verbally." Pearl said it perfectly. Her voice expressed the obvious, "Why would anyone want to surveil your car and you?"

"Oh wait, that whole big brother thing watching your every movement, listening to your phone, complete tracking of you to control you," Jeremy stepped it up a game. The room became solemn, dispirited.

"Let's go to the parks and walk around. Even though its cold outside it will be refreshing and Jeremy will get to see where Forrest sat on the bench and waited for his bus."

"Ready."

The twins joined them with a walk through several parks, shopping along the river and strolling through a couple graveyards. The air was brisk and it seemed like it might snow. Kristan got to know the twins some and found out they were adopted by their parents. She didn't explain that she was currently pregnant but asked polite questions about things she knew nothing about. They informed her and enlightened her about the whole thing. They loved their parents, respected them and didn't really think about being adopted except on rare occasions. Their parents talked openly and freely about the experience and even gave them a few pieces of information about the birth parents. That was good because Kristan decided she wanted to be known as the birth mother and would leave it open about future meetings. If it seemed right-then it would happen. If not-then no. This very small sense of control helped her, as though she wasn't losing everything, but all were gaining something important in their lives. She would have hope that her future would be hers yet to be fulfilled without 24/7 burdens, a family would become complete, a baby would know love and down the road both birth parents would know and be bonded by this forever, whether they were around each other or not. Her decision, her body, her baby ... she couldn't explain it but those thoughts calmed her. After speaking with the twins she knew she had made the right decision for all. On the way home it started snowing and Kristan felt blessed. Thank you Jesus for being in my life and to her angel she prayed, "You're the best."

That night the group, except the twins who had to go to work then study for a test, picked out an Irish Pub close by. The place had a live band with loud music and dancing. It was Saturday night and they were ready to party like young folks like to do.

"Dress warm but be able to take your sweater off because inside may get hot." Pearl said.

"What time are we going?" Kristan asked.

"I'll go whenever y'all are ready. I am hungry so I plan to eat. They have food don't they?" Jeremy asked.

"Yes, Jeremy they have food but I can make ya a sandwich so you don't starve," Pearl said.

"Yes, I would like that." Jeremy joined Pearl in the kitchen and flirted with her. "So you like to dance, huh?"

"I love to dance. And you?"

"You'll have to teach me," Jeremy was smitten. He'd seen Pearl on the Facetime call and now in person he felt attracted to her in a big way.

"Sure thing. There are some special jigs to do, that the Irish do. It's been awhile but I learned 'em back in high school one summer."

"Really?"

"Yes, my parents took me to Ireland and I swear by the third night of going to pubs I was a pro." Pearl smiled because of the thought of Ireland pubs, and also, her parents were still alive then.

"Well, it's a date then," replied Jeremy. "Let me put something finer on."

Jeremy went in the bedroom and pulled out the sweater his mother had bought for him for Christmas. It was black and fit perfectly. He put a cut undershirt on underneath. He didn't have big muscles but he was lean. He was pleased with his appearance and wore his black laced boots tonight. He brought a scarf and thought what the heck? The plaid added color to his black leather jacket. He didn't look so much like a college student but rather a young professional. He was glad he came to Savannah. He missed Kristan and she had asked him. They were friends and that was just fine. She'd just broken up with her long time high school boyfriend so she wasn't ready to date. But this Pearl was mesmerizing, fun, and very pretty, according to him. He'd ask Kristan tonight if she was dating anyone, or maybe he'd ask her himself.

Kristan wore a long black skirt with a fluffy sweater up top, under she had a long cotton top cut at each side. She could remove the top sweater if she got hot. She had ankle boots that zipped, a present from her mom and dad, and decided to put her hair up in an up do with long tendrils flowing around her face. She liked the look. Pretty soon in a couple months she wouldn't go out and she'd be a hermit, or maybe she'd go for walks on the beach she told herself in big sundresses with a coat.

Pearl, though, dressed for a date. She was a stunner in a dark green velvet mini dress with mesh stockings and shiny black high heels. She flat ironed her hair completely straight and applied her makeup like a pro.

"Wow ladies, let's go. We are going to have fun tonight!"

The threesome strode down East Oglethorpe Ave to Bull Street then followed East Congress Lane to O'Connell's Irish Pub. Arm in arm they went, the merriment with them, eating first at O'Connell's and then on to several other establishments for a bit of this and that, including some dance lessons for Jeremy. They found this pub that went below the street level and heard a band playing. The three settled there for the evening, dancing and drinking a couple beers.

"I noticed you're not drinking tonight Kristan," said Jeremy, "You feeling okay?"

"Thought I'd be the sober one to escort my friend's home, even if we are walking," she replied.

"Not that you have to to have a goodtime. But I do know you like white wine and beer."

She realized she needed to tell someone, someone who knew and respected her. And so she told Jeremy the story in warp speed. "Jeremy, I'm pregnant."

"Kristan! Oh, okay," he said.

"I'm okay. I'm keeping this secret but Pearl knows. I'm coming back to Vista after the baby is born."

"You are? Great, I look forward to that. And the baby?'

"I'm going to place the baby for adoption. I'm figuring that out in the next couple of months. I'm very sure about my plans. But please keep the secret until I return."

He got up and hugged her. This display was touching. Then he escorted Pearl to the dance floor. Not another word about babies was said.

Pearl was a good teacher holding Jeremy and moving him to and fro. The pair was relentless dancing cheek to cheek or swirling the partner around in place. Pearl placed Jeremy's hand on her waist and the other on her shoulder and told him to follow her footsteps. The spontaneous kiss at the end lasted a few seconds longer and the pair went for another drink at the table smiling broadly. They checked on Kristan who was playing with her phone.

"I'm fine. I'm enjoying the dance show. Keep it up for a while yet, then we'll go."

Chapter 19). Jeremy Dances and Returns Home

The snow came down lightly as the trio walked home with Jeremy in the center. What a fun night. Kristan felt energized as did Jeremy and Pearl. She remembered the kiss at the end of one dance. She put her head on Jeremy's shoulder and he squeezed his arm around her waist just enough to notice. Many people were out walking around going from place to place on a Saturday night. Christmas decorations were gone now but the snow became magical on this wintry night. It also quieted the outside noises. Snow did that-it made everything secondary. Once inside Kristan went right to bed. Pearl said goodnight to her and said she'd be in soon.

Pearl stood over by the family room window and watched the snow fall. Jeremy came over and looked outside with her. They stood there side by side eyeing nature in one of its most beautiful forms. Jeremy leaned over and kissed Pearl. She kissed him back in a long embrace. He took her hand and led her into her room. He closed the door behind them. He led her to her very own bed kissing her allowing her to retreat or stop at any moment but she didn't. She knew she would not go far but she wanted to kiss and cuddle with this man before her.

They tangled upon the bed rolling and exploring each other. This felt right and good. He kissed her neck and breasts while her heart felt the tenderness. The blinds were open and the light, heightened by the white snow, shone bright upon them in her bed. After an interlude of kissing and foreplay the couple fell asleep entangled in an interloping mix of limbs and minds. The calmness outside became one with two young souls in Savannah after meeting twenty four hours earlier. They awakened in the early morning, covered themselves, cuddled and remained under clothed.

When morning did come with the light of day Kristan told them she felt like staying in bed and talking on the phone with her mother. Jeremy said he was leaving around two o'clock. Pearl and Jeremy went out for a big breakfast down by the river. They made their way to River Street and ate at Two Cracked Eggs ordering the Crab Cake Benedict and Shrimp & Grits. Every savory bite was relished.

"Would you like anything more? I see you two were very hungry. Might I suggest a strawberry crepe to split?"

Jeremy looked at Pearl who smiled. "We would love that. Thank you."

The conversation on the walk back to her place was small talk about families, degrees, working or not, and where they came from. The weather was perfect. The snow stayed covering the ground as it had been cold several days prior. Many people were not out or were at church this morning. The street was quiet. The talk was consistent and inquisitive learning about one another. If music had been playing one would have called it joyous. Savannah was pretty with many old buildings nestled into each other, some fixed up others not. There was a sense of uniqueness and pride in this city. Like it had been something and was becoming something again. Pearl had been here since last August and had learned much since walking around herself. She told him about the waving girl statue at the river and the Girl Scout beginnings as well. And it had the best parade on Saint Patrick's Day which she hadn't seen yet, and don't forget about the movie Forrest Gump she reminded him.

"I should come again, I think," he said.

"You should. We could all go to the big old church-it's so beautiful inside and out."

"Yeah, I'd like that. Well, I'll be leaving. Let me give you my number, okay?"

"Sure. Take mine too," she replied.

Jeremy left and the winter day continued. It was gray, cold and covered in a white blanket. Both girls studied at their computers as classes were online this semester. For now the world appeared colorless from snow but soon the appendages of American life that would be discolored to gray from the covid virus of 2020 would appear as the virus rolled in. Everyone would be tired of covid and ready to resume an open life again later in the year.

Pearl went to the bathroom as she felt an intense cramp. She was at least ten days out from her surgery and the bleeding had been very slight. Minimal bleeding. That was good but she did feel a cold coming on, or maybe it was the flu. She went to bed to rest. She thought about getting a job as she couldn't get all the classes she had wanted. The next morning she checked out jobs online and applied to several. Later that day one responded and they were doing interviews. She didn't recognize the address but responded by email. They emailed back with an address and time to show up.

Kristan went to the grocery store around the corner and bought a couple bags worth for both of them. The twins went to another swim meet for their little sister-they would be gone all week. Classes were online. Pearl got ready for her interview-it was a bookkeeping job in a warehouse. She drove as it was a few miles away. The interview went well and Pearl got the job, the hours would be part time. The boss was new to town and asked if she wanted to attend a small party. She could bring her friends or roommates. Really, it was just a meet and greet. She said yes and likely would bring her roommate. Why not? Privately she wondered if Kristan would come to something like this.

Pearl texted Kristan the address for a small party. It was near the warehouse where her interview was. Pearl had some errands so she asked Kristan to take an Uber or Lyft. A couple hours later Kristan arrived and didn't see anyone. Was she at the right place? The Uber driver sped off. Kristan pulled out her phone and texted Pearl. No response. So she called her and let it ring. Someone else was talking on the other end.

"Who is this?" a man's voice asked.

"Who is this?" Kristan repeated.

"It's Pearl's friend," said the voice.

"Can I speak to her?" She pleaded.

"Ah, she asked me to watch her phone for her." The man looked out and saw her friend. "She's up the stairs, inside."

Kristan saw the stairs and headed for them. She slowed for a second or two, not sure if things were okay, but then sped forward to find her friend. Pearl was probably in the bathroom. She climbed the outside stairs which led to a second story business, warehouse, or even maybe a residence. She wasn't sure. She knocked and a man answered. He pulled her in.

"What's going on?"

"Let me ask the questions."

"Where's Pearl?" As soon as she asked she realized this guy was up to something. But what?

"She's having a little dream right now."

"Dream?"

"Yeah, you want one?"

"What? Is she laying down? Where?"

"She owes me money. So I guess you owe me money."

"Are you her new boss?"

"Boss? Oh that's what she was doing down here. She said she was at an interview and somebody would see me."

"Pearl," Kristan yelled out loud. She looked around and saw a door. He grabbed her arm and held her hurting her. "Let me see her, then I'll give you some money. How much?"

Kristan could only think to get her and get out of there. What if she couldn't walk? She'd have to call someone. Think. Think. Faster.

"I think you need some too." He grabbed her purse and looked for her wallet.

Quickly, she picked up the purse minus the wallet, the syringe he laid on the table, and ran to the closest door, opened it and closed it as fast she could. He must have been counting the money is why he didn't haste after her. She called 911 and gave them her address, description of the building, 2nd floor and all. She didn't know how Pearl was at the moment but figured she was close by. She looked at the syringe, wondered what it was, maybe the police would know. Maybe that's what he gave Pearl but why? Pearl probably didn't have any money on her. She said she was low on cash recently. He hadn't knocked on the door-possibly, he ran off. Then she heard the police sirens. She would open the door after they came up to this room. Her heart started racing-she hoped Pearl was okay. Her hands were sweaty now. She needed to know.

"Police," one of them opened the door from the outside. Kristan heard a scuttle and remained quiet.

She kept listening as the two were apparently getting control of each other. Then she heard another officer help the first one.

The second officer spoke to the first one. "Anyone else here?"

"In here. I called 911."

"Okay. We are securing the area. It will be safe soon." The police still had his gun drawn making sure.

Kristan opened the door slowly and showed her face before coming all the way out. "Did you get him, the guy?"

"Yes, he's taking him to the car in handcuffs."

"My friend is here somewhere-we must find her. It's likely he gave her this. He wanted money and was going to inject me with this. I have no idea why."

The police officer looked at it and secured it in a glove. "You stay with me in case there are others. The backup will look for her. Do you think she's on this floor?"

"I do because he used her phone and I was close by walking to meet her."

"I found her," an officer said down the hall and in another room.

Kristan put her hands to her mouth, frightened to hear any more words. "She's okay, I got a pulse and a low respiratory rate."

"Let me call an ambulance," the officer attending Kristan said.

"Let me see her, please," she begged. And so he did. He walked her into the other room.

Pearl was pale, barely breathing, and unconscious. Kristan felt light headed and proceeded to pass out.

"Oh, no, another one down." He called his partners.

The ambulance arrived and put oxygen on Pearl immediately. They quickly checked her blood pressure and it was extremely low. They started an IV and put her on a stretcher and took her to the hospital by ambulance. The other emergency tech attended Kristan, telling them she was pregnant and she would be fine. They told her what hospital Pearl would go to. Kristan sat there with the officer and drank a cool drink. Then she walked with him and he drove her to the hospital to see Pearl. He made sure she was fine sitting in the waiting room, told the staff and left for the precinct to give them the drug and test it. He had a feeling what it might be but waited. The ER docs attended Pearl and the staff stayed close to her. Later that night the police officer returned to tell Kristan what had likely happened and what the drug turned out to be. She thanked him for coming back with the update and was so glad he rescued both of them.

"He's a drug dealer but they weren't his drugs. He stole them to make some quick easy money but couldn't find anyone to buy them. So he saw Pearl and gave her a dose, injected it himself but then she had no money. It's a good thing you came when you did, took the injection and called us. You saved both of your lives," he said.

Kristan practically passed out again. She shook her head, drank the water before her and took it all in. All because they were headed to a party they never made it to. Wrong place at the wrong time reverberated in her thoughts. She guessed they were staying in the rest of the winter.

"Pearl will be all right. The fentanyl slows your breathing and if given too much, stops it, then your heart stops and you can die if not treated immediately. It's a dangerous drug used for pain medication in the hospital and patients undergoing surgery or medical procedures."

"I've actually heard of it."

The officer gave her a small hug. She'd been through a rough day and there was no family nearby. "You okay?"

"Yes. I'll stay here until she can leave. I'll take her home. Actually, I need to pick up her car."

"I can take you so you can drive it back here to wait for

her."

"Good thing. I'd like some protection in that area where it's parked."

Chapter 20). Pearl and Kristan Bonding

Both girls slept and stayed inside for two days. On the third day the pair united on the sofa. They were still by themselves as the twins were gone for a week visiting their parents at an out of state swim meet.

"It's nearly February, Pearl. I'm beginning to show. See," Kristan said and held her bare belly.

"Just a bit, not much."

"Are you showing, yet? And did they say everything would be okay at the hospital?"

"There's nothing to show Kristan."

"What do you mean?"

"Nada."

"You lost the baby?"

"No. I have something to tell you, though."

"We're friends. You can tell me anything. You know I don't have many friends and I'm glad we met. It was a meant to be thing, ya know?"

"I agree. It was a meant to be thing. But the situation has changed. Please don't be mad. Promise."

"Of course, I promise."

"I had an abortion," she said the words and sat there

waiting for a response if a response was required.

Kristan looked at her and the inside of her brain wanted to tumble that information like a dishwasher, clean it, dry it, and make it new. But that didn't happen. Her words spoken forth were genuine and heartfelt.

"Oh Pearl, that's what you had to do. It must have been difficult, the burden, to not be ready and make such a big decision. I wish I could have been there for you like you have been for me."

Pearl knew her brand new friend would say the most beautiful thing. And she did. Tears rolled down her cheeks and she went over to hug her friend.

"We are friends. You are the best. Thank you. Thank you."

"You're welcome."

"I went and prayed after I did it. Maybe, I should have prayed before. But God helps those who help themselves and I asked for forgiveness and he understood. Now you make me feel whole, like I'm an okay person, not a bad person."

"Do not judge, lest ye be judged, is one of the finest examples of kindness and humanness around, I think, straight from God or Jesus."

"I will continue to help you with this pregnancy and ultimate adoption. You are one brave person Miss Kristan.

You might just be a role model for the right to lifers," Pearl exclaimed.

"I'm somewhat mixed on this issue. I'm for life but allowances for an early abortion, whereas, late term must be baby and mother ill health related. I'm beginning to like the heart beat bill as a measure for women to not procrastinate further and a reminder to use protection. But look at us-we didn't."

"Because we are imperfect and God knows that."

"I feel okay with my decision." Pearl admitted.

"I would like to go to church with you sometime. Is it that big old Catholic Church?" Kristan questioned.

"Yes. It is. Jeremy wants to come too."

"Okay, next time he comes let's all go."

"Cool. Perfect date." They laughed lightly.

They talked. They made lunch. They napped. They ordered delivery for dinner. They even had a glass of wine.

"I have something for you. I bought it a few days ago. Let me get it." Pearl left the room. She had almost forgotten the baby gift she had purchased and wrapped.

"What a wonderful day," whispered Kristan. She had a friend and they swapped stories. Both were on the same path just different outcomes. She was still happy with her decision. Pearl would help her along the way. Her mom, too.

Pearl walked in with a large bag overflowing with tissue wrapping. "Here. I hope you like it."

Kristan smiled and opened her gift. She hadn't thought about presents. She would miss out on that. But here was Pearl helping her to not miss out on that. The first present was a maternity sundress.

"Beautiful, look at this. I'm going to wear it every day." The second present was for the baby. A snuggly white onesie with little pink lambs, blue skies and a big yellow sun over top. She put her hand to her stomach. "This baby will always be a part of both of our lives, I declare it right here Pearl. It's learning already about love and friendship." She hugged her friend, then thanked God for bringing her such a good friend.

"In the spring when you are big, and wearing your dress, we'll go out for a fancy tea with all three!" Pearl swirled her arm to include all of them.

"Yes. Bless you." Kristan walked over to the kitchen calendar and went to the month of May, circling Mother's Day with a heart. "This day will be perfect."

Chapter 21). Investigator Goes on a Ghost Tour

The months went by, the girls studied, the twin's sister did earn a full scholarship to Auburn University for swimming. Everyone was pleased and spring had sprung in Savannah. They skipped St. Patty's Day and celebrated with take out. Kristan was still working at the Ghost Tours during the day a few days a week. Her mom was coming soon for a visit and Pearl had found a job in an office for a building company. She caught quite a few colds this winter and her color had not returned but she assured Kristan she was well. Today Kristan had a few VIP's in attendance. She didn't recognize their names but was told they were government officials.

She had the tour memorized and was able to add in tidbits as the company allowed. That made for a more exciting and memorable tour. Her tour went down streets talking about history, that and grave yards, and ended inside an old historic home privately owned. It was almost like an arcade with fans blowing wind inside the rooms, some heated, some with cool air. It stirred the appetite for a hands on experience, almost like Halloween. Her tour was the newest one in Savannah. Even a mist blew outside that was like raindrops from Heaven. All in all she had a good time every day. At the end of her tour sandwiches were served outside with a courtyard seating. Drinks were served along with a few Georgia delicacies such as pralines.

"What's a praline?" one might ask her.

And she'd say, "Wait until the end and order one. You will love it. Nothing like it in all the world."

The VIP tour went well and the group of seven persons asked quite a few questions. Kristan thought she handled it pretty well. The group was very excited about the courtyard with southern sandwiches, drinks and snacks for purchase. At the conclusion they could sit out back under a large southern oak with Spanish moss and contemplate their next move. They seemed to be on a business vacation.

"Actually, it's a meeting. What's your name again?" asked the lady with medium brown highlighted hair.

"I'm Kristan. I'm a college student here in Georgia."

"Nice to meet you. I'm Kim from Georgia running for Congress," she gave her last name and county but Kristan didn't take it all in like she should have.

"Nice to meet you too," Kristan said. "You look familiar like I've met you before."

"I think I know your mother, Chloe," she said.

"Oh, yes. You lost your twin a few years ago. I'm so sorry," Kristan said. "My mom and I saw you in Valdosta."

"I did lose my sister and thank you. That's right, last fall you all were out to lunch at the Magenta Fleurs Café. You know, tomorrow we have off to go around and enjoy the city as we please. Maybe you'd like to have lunch with me.

I'm learning from the young people what they want in the world and I'd like to ask you some questions. Are you available?"

Kristan was honored that someone cared about what she thought about.

"As it goes I'm completely free tomorrow, no classes, no ghost tours, and no dates, except yours. I would love to!"

"Perfect. We have a car at our disposal so we'll pick you up. I thought we would really go classy and do some Capital Club type restaurant-so dress nice." Kim explained.

"What time?"

"How about 12 noon?"

"I'll be ready. It's a date," Kristan hoped she didn't sound too excited but she was thrilled to be going to lunch with someone who knew everything, or at least she thought she did."

"Pearl," she screamed.

"What on earth is the matter? You okay?"

"No. I mean, yes, I'm fine. I'm having lunch tomorrow with a congresswoman elect, or a hopeful anyway," she managed to explain in full detail.

"Oh, wow. Okay. Let's get you prepped. Let me get on my computer."

"What?"

"You don't want to go and act all dumb and foolish like a freshman, do you?"

"Great point, let's get studying."

Kristan herself looked up how many people were in Congress and how many from each state and did the same for senators. She had to know what she was talking about. After educating herself, Pearl ascribed her friend to know the hot topics of the day and there were many. The two rehearsed situations, conversations and viewpoints.

The places she'd be going could be Elizabeth on 37th, The Collins Quarter, Capital Grille, or Pearl's Saltwater Grille, The Grey, Vinnie Van GoGo's, The Olde Pink House, Fox and Fig Cafe, Atlantic, even The Lady and Sons. Kristan could hardly sleep. What should she say or not say?

Kristan was five months pregnant and could still fit in her one and only suite she had. Pearl helped her to alter the waist. Perfect. She looked the part of a professional student near graduation. Ha. She was a freshman. But today she would be important. And off she went to a fancy lunch with a future congresswoman. She remembered something very important her mother used to tell her. Ask the person you're with about themselves-this tactic warms them to you and they are butter in your mouth. That must have come from some farm is all she could think. But it was good advice so one doesn't just talk about themselves. Rules of Engagement, wasn't that a book title? Okay. She thought, I'm nervous.

A long black SUV waited at the curb, the kind the government travels in all the time while in motorcades or caravans for important business, while a driver came to the door. Answering the door she followed him and then he opened the door for her to step in. She did. As soon as she did she was welcomed by Kim. No need to worry about conversation as this lady did all the talking, ten minutes later she had her laughing and engaging like they were sisters.

"I really needed to chat with someone who isn't fighting for this or that. Politicians have a hard time agreeing. You are the welcome change."

"Thanks. I think," Kristan said.

"Now we go to lunch and I'll let you talk. Think about the worries of young college students, girls in particular," Kim issued.

Kristan was given a choice and the two ladies could hardly decide between two restaurants. She said, "It's decided, we'll have lunch at one and dessert at the other."

Over lunch she asked her two questions and they discussed strategies about how it could be fixed. When dessert came at the other place the topic became more personable. The topic became what girls have to struggle with from sex, to college classes and more, even abortion vs. pregnancy. When the discussion was almost over

Kristan shared with her her personal journey but made her promise it was for her ears only. Now she had told three people, make that five including her parents.

"Thank you for sharing that. Not in a million years did I expect to talk about this, and you know firsthand the struggles for which you are engaged in, they are your struggles alone."

"You're welcome," Kristan acknowledged her small part.

"May I call you or discuss with you again to see how you manage with the birth and outcome. I very much would like to stay in touch."

They talked more.

"Kristan, I actually know a couple looking to adopt that live in Florida over near the Gulf of Mexico. A wonderful couple with three boys who are looking to make their family larger by one more child. They both are wonderful parents, loving, playful, all the good stuff. She just told me the other day. I could connect you both."

"I would like that. A recommendation would be fine as I'd like to know I could someday be a small part of the family to see the child in their lives."

"She mentioned the same thing. I'd like to give you a card with their names and phone number. You could call and talk about everything. No pressure."

"Thank you."

"No thank you," Kim said. "When are you due?"

"The first week in June, June 6th," she explained.

"Towards the end of May I'll be on an investigative trip coming back down here near the Florida Georgia line followed by a trip to the Gulf-I could take you there. By that time you would need someone to be with you all the time. Run that by your mother when she comes next week. I just want to help. I don't want to overrun you with details," said Kim.

Kristan smiled. Many things seemed to be falling in place. "I'm so glad you asked me to lunch. I hope I helped you with some questions about young college students, costs, classes, and other issues."

"You did. Tremendously," said Kim.

Kristan took the card and said she be in touch. The timing was perfect as she had put that on the list for March or April.

The congresswoman elect had won her party but required a special primary runoff. She would be installed in her new position if she won in two months was wowed by a college student. She didn't expect all that professionalism and adultism to be prevalent in an 18 or 19 year old. Her car drove away. She'd be back down here the end of May investigating a tip she'd received about spying and surveillance. She had to do this herself, firsthand, otherwise, politicians wouldn't believe anyone, and they'd twist it to favor their party. This had to be nonparty, nonpolitical, and for the people. Even if she was an outsider she wanted to get this information into the right hands. She'd be back and maybe Kristan would travel with her to her final destination, Destin. Rather incredible that the very conversation ended with a possibility for her friends in the Gulf. Obviously, many couples who experience infertility would love a chance to adopt a baby from birth, to be given a chance at a family of their own. She wanted to eventually highlight this act of bravery and selflessness in a young person. Kim thought this is the beauty in the world not everyone sees which makes living worthwhile.

Meant to be ... is all Kristan could think of. She smiled and took a long nap post 'the greatest lunch ever.'

Chapter 22). Kristan's Mom Visits

Pearl had to go to court and give testimony to what happened to her two months ago. She told herself she could do it. The drug dealer slash pusher slash potential murderer was going to get a stiff sentence the police and prosecutor told her and with her statements the deal would be sealed. He was stupid, careless and didn't think that her life could have been ended that night. The amount of narcotic was double what druggies normally give, therefore it was meant for two people to share per a needle. People still did that. She thought places gave out needles to junkies preventing people from getting HIV and AIDS.

Hell, what did she know she didn't run in that world? How could she know? She was walking along that night after her interview, she parked and realized she had the wrong address and the place must have been around back. Wrong place wrong time. The loser saw her and BAM before she knew it he had her inside the building. She was out of cash, because that's what he really wanted, and then brazenly he gave her the shot but before he did, Pearl told him her friend was coming and she'd have some money. He waited for her friend and was going to do the same thing to her. Kristan grabbed the shot, her purse minus the wallet he'd pulled out and bolted for the bathroom. Breathless but hardened for the moment she dialed 911 and called it in. He counted the money while she did this. This gave her time and appeased him, momentarily. The cops came quickly with backup. An unfortunate situation quickly turned responsive by law professionals and Kristan's brave quick actions at the right time. Pearl was able to give her testimony in closed quarters with both attorneys and the judge. After almost losing her life no further stress was added to her situation. She was glad about that.

Pearl walked from the courthouse back home. She strolled leisurely looking at the big old houses and the blossoms. The fuchsia colored azaleas were abundant everywhere one looked and now the dogwoods nestled among and above them grabbed the spotlight. Their limbs climbed in search of the truth. What was the truth? The sunlight of course. By mid-April the climax would be reached for this glorious sight which Savannah was privy to on a yearly basis. Pearl reveled in the flowers and wondered what her future looked like. She had to decide on a major fairly soon with her studies. She liked her new job, maybe she should get into the building industry, or become an architect. She thought about the architect idea. That would mean an office high-rise looking out at some big city. Yeah, that excited her. But she did love the country as her folks were from Kentucky and had a small farm. Why couldn't one have both? She kept walking and picked up a sandwich to take home. Kristan's mother would be here soon and all this would be over. Pearl liked her new friend and didn't want to lose that. She would need to visit her at Vista next fall for a weekend.

Chloe attended the doctor's appointment with her daughter and all was set. Her health and the baby were fine. No problems whatsoever he said. She should have a healthy baby and didn't expect any delivery issues. Kristan made him aware of her destination and he found a doctor there for her. She would need to be there 10-14 days prior to delivery date for safety. That was her plan. Kristan asked him his thoughts about her plans and did he have any recommendations about family and visits in the future. He recommended an open plan for communication and to pull back if needed. Usually, if one is told from the beginning it works well because of no surprises. Children all react differently and settle into themselves at different times. Everybody thinks there is this normal timeline built with ideas of perfection. We are not that anymore but some still want the ideal. I believe it's changing. But give the child time to process on their timeline. It might never be a problem or one might be in first grade talking all about it. One mother who adopted twins was asked in third grade from the back seat, "Mommy, were we in your tummy at the same time?" She'll tell the child according to his or her age. My one and only suggestion is to not lie or tell them so late in age like when they are a teenager. This is too much drama so late in the game. You can talk with the adoptive mother about these kinds of things.

"Best to you, here's the doctor's name. She is expecting your call. I've told her all about you and sent the sonograms as well," the doctor said.

"Thank you. I feel relieved," Kristan said.

"Me, too," said her mother.

He smiled at them and they left.

"Lunch?" asked Chloe.

"Burger, shake and fries. Big fries with vinegar and ketchup!"

"Okay, if that's what you are craving."

"Yes. I've been eating so healthy. Pearl cooks healthy all the time with salads, homemade soup and chicken, lots of chicken. I need a cheeseburger."

"Let's go down by the river it's such a nice day."

"Do you suppose I wimped out, mom?"

"What do you mean, honey?"

"Like should I have told the father, or had an abortion, or maybe even kept the baby?" Kristan had a moment of distress, right after the doctor's appointment.

"Honey, it's okay to question the decisions one makes in life, especially, right before we are about to execute them. This is natural, let's eat, you nap, and you'll be back to normal. I support everything you are doing. You, yourself, said you would be telling him this year. I'm good with that. I like that you made a plan, it's natural, loving and the baby will have a home with two parents who are stable. God's looking out for you. I mean that."

"Thanks. Let's eat."

Mother and daughter had a good day down by the river on a Spring Day in Savannah. It was actually fun. Kristans mind cleared and she was back to herself thinking positively about her plan. She told her mom all about the phone call with the couple. They talked for two hours the other night-they learned about each other and in the end all was calm. They would talk or Facetime every two weeks until she arrived the last week of May.

"You've been in touch with Kim and she's going to drive you to the Gulf?"

"Yes, we will stop somewhere for three days on the way and celebrate Memorial Day, then we head right there. A week after the birth I'll head home. I hope I don't get all weepy but I guess that can happen to women who give birth. Did you?"

"No, I didn't. I was young and I started taking a dance class, jazz, which helped with everything in getting the body back to normal, head, mind and muscles."

"That's good advice. Take a class with me this summer, and say yes."

"Yes, I will." Her mother was very proud of her daughter. Unbelievably proud.

Chapter 23). Winded and Sick Pearl Drives Herself to the Hospital

Pearl woke up late and called in sick. It was true when she got out of bed and walked to the kitchen her breath became winded. Was she getting another flu? Maybe she should go back to that clinic and ask them if everything is all right. Her parents were both dead but neither of them had any issues that she knew about. She sat down and drank some orange juice, followed by an English muffin. She poured a cup of coffee and went to her bedroom. She laid upon her bed after she closed the door looking around at her walls. Her job was great, she was changing her major and she loved her roommates. All things considered it didn't get better than this. She would know as the first year was horrendous with the girls she roomed with. Out all night, no studying and trying this and that. This year was so different. Kristan had come into her life and their shared experience brought a bond-even though she ended her part she was there to help her new friend. She sipped her coffee and then got up to go to the bathroom. She felt lightheaded and slipped to the floor. No one was home so no one would hear her.

Later when she came to she rose slowly and got her balance. She knew she wasn't pregnant-so what was this? Must have been something she ate last night, except her stomach was not bothered. She laid back on the bed and noticed her ankles. They were bigger than normal. That's when she looked at her hands. Her hands were whiter than usual and her fingernails were dusky, not blue but whitish.

She noticed she was almost out of breath just walking around her bedroom.

Pearl could take a nap and see how she felt later on. But in light of that medical procedure and the drug injection by a druggie that she almost died from, she decided to immediately go to the hospital. She packed a bag and drove herself as no one was home. She didn't want to bother anyone. She probably needed an antibiotic, maybe something stayed inside her and was making her ill. She had had several flu and cold like symptoms these past two months. The Emergency Room was great when they brought her there for the narcotic overdose, so it's there she drove to as quickly as possible.

When she walked in they remembered her and treated her like royalty. They had told her she was lucky to have survived and her friend, as well as the police, had saved her life. The nurse walked her into a room and helped her to lay upon the bed in there. She let her say her troubles while she took her vital signs. Usually, one gets the vitals in a room next to the waiting room but the nurse could see her distress. She was noticeably short of breath, pale and somewhat weak. Immediately after the vital signs the nurse helped her to put a hospital gown on and inserted nasal cannula O2 in her nostrils. She told her this would help her.

Next up she hooked her to the EKG monitor to get her heart rate and look for arrhythmias. An automatic blood pressure cuff recorded her blood pressure every ten minutes. The blood pressure was near normal but the heart rate was accelerated with an occasional PVC, or premature ventricular contraction. She listened to her chest, both lungs, and noted absence of breath sounds bilaterally in the mid to distant fields. She took a short bio, turned on the alarms and went to retrieve the ER doctor. Certain patients get seen faster than others and this was the case with Pearl. It's called triage and nurses do this every day in hospitals across America, especially, in the emergency rooms. The nurse went out and ordered an x-ray knowing that would be tops on the list along with other blood work. Pearl smiled at the doctor, she was trying to see if he was concerned. If he was he showed no signs, unlike her signs which pointed in a grave direction. He didn't want to tire her out so he held off a few questions until after the chest x-ray. He did note she told him she'd had a few colds and flu these past two months. This information tore at him but he held back for the x-ray and blood gases he'd ordered. As soon as he had the x-ray, and if confirmed, he'd call the cardiologist.

He didn't want to jump to conclusion but he didn't like her skin, her breathing and the ankles with pitting edema. He read her chart from the last visit two months earlier while he waited for the x-ray.

The nurse helped with the x-ray and made her comfortable with an extra blanket warmed by the warmer down the hall. This is the best hospital thought Pearl. Everyone was quick and attentive. Simply the best place she'd ever been. They were all so professional. In a little while she would call Kristan to tell her where she was. Maybe after the x-ray she'd know more of what was going on.

She gave the nurse Kristan's number of who to call since she had no family. She was all alone in the world, except for an uncle she never saw any more and it didn't bother her. It had been that way since she was seventeen. She was used to it by now.

The nurse left. She saw her over by the doctor. They were viewing her x-ray. Come tell me I'm okay and that I need some antibiotics for all these colds I'm getting. She braced herself for another IV with fluids and maybe staying a day. She was not ready for the serious nature of doctor and nurse walking in like they'd seen a ghost or been on the tour downtown.

The sterile man and woman who came in said nothing for a few moments. Then the doctor held up the x-ray and put it on the light board in the room. He looked at her and spoke softly but directly. "Pearl," he started.

"Yes, doctor," she replied.

"Your heart is quite enlarged."

"Yes, I have a big heart. That's a good thing, right?"

He stopped. "No, Pearl, that is not good. In fact, it could be dangerous and very grave. You need to be admitted and seen by a cardiologist."

"Okay." She said this slowly looking at the nurse.

"You need to be watched and monitored in the ICU."

"Oh, very serious."

"The cardiologist is going to meet you up there. You will be comfortable and the nurses are the best as they deal with situations like this all the time. They are the best in the city. Anywhere, for that matter."

"I need to call my friend Kristan," Pearl realized the seriousness but wasn't scared.

"I'll write some orders, medication for comfort, and the doctor will see you up there. I've spoken with her."

"Doctor, why is my heart so big?"

"That is what we will have to find out. Sometimes it's hereditary, sometimes it comes on from a medical condition, or even a virus."

"Does it go away?" she had to ask.

"Sometimes it can, or it can be treated medically. On rare occasion a person has a heart transplant."

She waved him off with a goodbye hand. She didn't want to hear that word like some sci fi experiment, or vampire wanting her dead. She texted Kristan where she was. Kristans mother had left today and now she was back at the apartment. She would come. She would pick up togo food. Could she eat? She didn't tell her she was going to the intensive care unit where Dracula performed death miracles or they put a string on your toe and shoved you to the morgue. She became nervous. She closed her eyes and waited. She dreamed. She explored. She was headed for another planet, the one with all the tubes and gadgets for coma patients.

Her windedness had dispersed with the nasal cannula added. Her nailbeds were no longer dusky, even her hands had a pink color now. They wheeled her right in the bed up to the intensive care unit. Once there they transferred her to another bed, several nurses assisted and she was hooked up to more monitors. The doctor did indeed meet her there and told her what tests she was going to order for her to see how severe her condition. She assured her everyone would take excellent care of her. By tomorrow she would formulate a plan and know much, much more. If Pearl thought of anything just ask the nurses they can tell you what you need to know. She also said if her friend could come by tomorrow she could give her an update, too.

Later that night after a couple scans Kristan showed up and had some takeout food with her. "I better ask the nurses if you can have this. I'll be right back."

It was dark now and Pearl was tired out. "What did they say?"

"Yes, you can eat this. Its two mini burgers. They said to

be sure to follow it with a drink. Your tests are complete and none are ordered for the morning so you can drink and eat."

"I guess I'll be taking a sleeping pill tonight with all these constant noises and beeps going off."

"Yes. Do that. Pearl, I can't believe you drove yourself to the hospital being all winded and pale."

"I'll be all right. I think it's serious but nothing some antibiotics can't undo. Don't worry."

Pearl was reassuring Kristan who was definitely showing now. Kristan was hungry all the time with a baby kicking half the time and now her best friend was in the ICU. She told herself to call Jeremy. He would calm all of them. She said goodbye. Said she'd see her in the morning and leant over to kiss her forehead. She wasn't sure why she did that. The situation looked like it called for an emotional goodbye, a symbol of her love. She gave it freely.

Chapter 24). Pearl in the ICU

In the morning, before any friends arrived, Pearls doctor ordered a Foley catheter to catch all her urine and told her she was giving her huge amounts of Lasix to diurese and flush out her kidneys. This would make her heart work less and give it a break. She had studied her scans and her situation was very serious, almost grave. Did she know what that was?

"No, I don't."

"Pearl. It is so severe I'm going to put you on the heart transplant list. A new healthy heart is likely the only way for you to survive this."

"If I just rest maybe it can un stretch and go back to normal."

"You may get some cardiac output back, even slight may help. Unfortunately, it's just not sustainable for a life going forward. I wish I had better news."

Her voice quivered and her eyes welled up. "Are you sure?"

"Yes. My hope is that we can find a heart for you in the next week or two, if not earlier."

The nurse came in and gave her the Lasix, then drew some blood from the arterial line. She sent this off to the lab. The nurse seemed to sense how dire the situation really was at this moment in Pearl's life. "Your friend has arrived. Are you ready to see her?"

The doctor spoke with Kristan and she gave her a card to call for anything. Kristan walked to the door and stepped into Pearl's room on the second floor.

"Hi."

"Hi."

Kristan sat down and held her friends hand.

They sat in silence taking in the severity of the moment. This day. This place.

"I called Jeremy. He's coming to see you."

"Oh, Jeremy, that will be wonderful." The room was full of equipment, monitors, the large ICU bed, oxygen, IV's, a sink, a chair and a window to the world behind her. Her view was the door watching white coats and scrubs go by, minute after minute. What does a twenty year old female think about when two months ago she was pregnant, and now, here, laying in a hospital bed possibly dying? Kristan had no words and none were said. She held her hand for two hours and then kissed her forehead, touched her shoulder and said goodbye. She'd be back with Jeremy and they would tell stories tonight, the three of them.

Jeremy and Kristan arrived before dark and were allowed in for a visit. The nurse was busy emptying her Foley, which had lots of pee in it.

"That's a good thing they tell me. See... lots of pee," the three of them laughed a little and then laughed some more. Jeremy said his hellos and was sorry to see her here.

"What can I do for you Pearl? I'm so sorry about this, your condition. I'm devastated."

"Well, please turn my bed around so I can see out the window. I'd like to look at nature instead of medicine," she said and pointed behind her to the picture window taking up most of the wall.

Kristan and Jeremy asked the nurse and she didn't mind. In fact she helped them in this matter. The patient was on the transplant list waiting for a heart. If she didn't get one her time would not be long. Everyone knew this. There was absolutely nothing wrong with turning the bed 180 degrees, all was still connected and working. The patient smiled and was noticeably encouraged. The trio played little voice games, storytelling and tagging each other. The patient forgot how dire her situation, enjoyed herself and lived freely in her mind looking at the beautiful trees and the savannah marshland in the distance. She was thankful for her friends.

That night after the friends left the nurse came in the room and Pearl seemed to want to talk. The nurse took the time and gave her some minutes to express herself. She had no idea this would be the last time the nurse would see this very young patient who was deathly ill but one wouldn't really see that as it was all happening on the inside.

She told her how she lost her parents. She told her she had an abortion two months ago. And she told her she had been sick with the flu and a cold for a few weeks now. She had no idea it was so severe. She even drove herself to the hospital. Her car was parked right outside over there. Compassion in times of need is beauty for the heart. Pearl smiled and thanked the nurse for helping her friends to move the bed to see outside. All they did was swing the foot of the bed over keeping the head near all the important monitors.

The next morning some asshole doctor on call came in, not Pearl's doctor, and awakened Pearl by startling her and yelling about the bed. He demanded the nurses turn the bed back to face the door and then examined the patient. He was rough and rude and Pearl couldn't wait for him to leave. The nurse thought ... what does he have to prove? Where does he get off rearranging furniture? The nurse making rounds knew he wasn't a very good doctor making wrong diagnosis at times in the past. Why didn't somebody report him? In fact, she was going to do that after lunch she decided. His lack of caring was immense and destructive to the unit.

She never made it to the nurse managers' office to report the doctor's ill behavior in front of a patient. The patient in 216 with the red DNR sign on the door arrested and died. Peacefully. She didn't live to find a new heart, or look out the window again, and her friends were not there to see her to say good bye. But they had the night before made her life beautiful one last time by showing her the natural world and their loving hearts with beautiful funny stories.

Pearl's doctor called Kristan and told her how deeply saddened she was. A transplant would have helped but her condition had deteriorated even after the Lasix. There was little hope. Kristan just couldn't believe it. She asked why this happened to her.

The doctor explained, "What I can say is that she caught a virus and it went and settled into her heart then damaged the muscle causing the enlargement. The heart then functions at a minimum of what it can do. We call this cardiomyopathy and many times we are unsure of the cause. It didn't seem to be infectious as there was no temperature. Sometimes they call this Idiopathic Cardiomyopathy, we just don't know the cause. "

"She kept telling me she needed antibiotics."

"It was a virus which antibiotics will not cure. She was unlucky to be stricken, but lucky to have such sweet friends."

"Thank you."

"There's nothing you could have done. Her heart filled up that tiny little chest she had and it couldn't move. I'm so sorry. Call me for anything further."

"Goodbye."

"Goodbye."

Jeremy and Kristan walked in her apartment and Kristan went to her room and wept. And wept.

Chapter 25). The Funeral

Kristan made arrangements with the hospital and through phone coordination with a very distant relative in Kentucky. No one would be able to attend-so it was Kristan, her recent coworkers, the twins and some other school friends that would hold a ceremony. Jeremy said he'd be there with plenty of tissues. Said he'd help with whatever she needed. Kristan drove Pearl's car to the big church near downtown, the very one Pearl had prayed in. She wanted someone to attend and say a few words. She wanted to attend a service there to feel Pearl's presence she supposed. One thing Pearl had said in one of many conversations the two of them had that cremation was fine with her ... ashes to ashes dust to dust, better for the environment and land. Plus she said I do not want to be a 'Walking Dead,' then she laughed.

The arrangements were finalized and it would be Mother's Day. Jeremy asked, "Are you sure?"

"No, I'm not sure, but neither of us is going to be a mother so let's celebrate and mourn this loss together. Pearl would think this the best idea ever. I can hear her saying it," Kristan said the truth.

The end of April came and Pearl's ashes arrived in a box. Kristan had purchased a nice vase and came up with an idea to honor her new friend. She was going to place Pearl's ashes in three places representing the body, mind and spirit. She'd keep a portion in the vase for herself in remembrance of her. She just had to. She had a feeling she would be praying to this person for a long time. That would cover the body, next the mind must go to the Gulf, where the new baby would reside-this would represent caring and watching over the life that goes on. Finally, the spirit was in Savannah. So to the river they'd go and slip in a few ashes, listen to some Irish music, and give a wave to the waving girl statue down by the water who says hello to all the boats coming in and goodbye to the ones leaving. This felt complete, this idea. Jeremy loved it when she told him on the phone. She thanked Jeremy and felt bonded to him through this experience. They were becoming closer than ever.

"See you Friday, the seventh." Jeremy said.

"And you can stay until Monday? Right?" she asked.

"Yes, do I need to order flowers for the dinner?"

""I'll cover that, the restaurant will be colorful due to Mother's Day, but our place will need some cheering. You can pay the priest, he's coming and said it would be $125 for the service."

"There's ten of us including the priest. That's a nice number. Everyone is coming to dinner too."

"Pearl had cashed her last three paychecks but hadn't spent the money. It was on her dresser and she told me to use it to have a celebration with you." Silence. Then choking and coughs. Followed by sucked in breaths and sorrowful tears with quiet, muted screams.

"I'm sorry Kristan. That should cover the dinner. We'll be okay sweetie. Thank you for being you. See you then, next week."

Kristan shook her head up and down as tears ran down her cheeks in thoughts of her friend Pearl. She couldn't utter any more words.

"Bye now," Jeremy said and hung up.

Kristan hung up the phone. She sat on the sofa and dreamt this nightmare in her mind with the reel of Pearl on repeat, laughing, fighting for her life, looking out the picture window at the end of her life. Kristan kept choking on her thoughts, as streams of tears flowed down both cheeks. She held her stomach stiffly.

The day had finally arrived. It seemed like seven lifetimes since Pearl had passed. Today it would be over after a celebratory ceremony and Mother's Day dinner, followed by a few footsteps to the river. Today would be light because since Friday the two lives who came into Pearl's life had been sorrowful, sad, and distracted with her death.

Ten people including the priest presiding over the formal ceremony at the church sat while a church pipe organ played above them.

"Ladies and gentlemen we are gathered here today ...," the priest began telling the small assembly of souls about life and death and where we go when we die. Then he added a few notes from what Kristan had described. He had also seen the young woman with porcelain skin praying one day in the middle of the day. That was a little unusual. "Pearl had recently visited the church and prayed. I remember her that day coming and staying for quite a while. God hears our prayers and helps us to be with him in faith and good measure. Pearl has gone to be with her parents, in the name of God."

The music played and then it was over. The vase was given back to Kristan and she and Jeremy decided to walk to the river before dinner.

"You look beautiful Kristan. I wish your mother was here to see you. I think she'd say the same."

"It's the dress."

"Pearl bought me this dress, this and a baby gift," she said. She twirled around.

"Such a short time knowing our friend and here we are mourning her. Do you suppose God puts people in your life to wake you up or show you the way?" Jeremy reflected and asked one of life's tough questions.

"Absolutely."

"Absolutely, what?"

"I think everything is a reflection. All of it."

"Go on."

"What you see you get, except for the catastrophes. They are like nature such as when a volcano erupts. It might kill people. It doesn't happen all the time, either. These catastrophes wake us up to appreciate and love, reminding us we are just little human beings. You know, the thing where they say, 'don't sweat the small stuff and it's all small stuff.' The volcano gets your attention. Pearl was a volcano, a beautiful hot explosion, making way for more life in the future. She was fertile, loving and our friend who had no family. Yet, she was happy."

"She touched us in a good way. And now we won't have her except for a memory. Maybe she'll be watching over us."

"That's nice, Jeremy."

"You know, I was starting to like her, to fall in love with her. I wanted to ask her out again, maybe start something," he said.

"Oh, I'm sorry. I know. But what does that tell you? Don't wait. Live. Live now."

He hugged Kristan tightly and when he released her he held out his hand for the vase.

He had a white handkerchief, or napkin from the restaurant and poured some ashes into it.

They were close by to the waving girl. They walked up to her and spilled some ashes out near her base, then they went to the closest tree and spilled some more. They had no idea what they were doing but it seemed the most natural thing to do.

The couple met the others for a special Mother's Day-Life Celebration dinner. Drinks were ordered, a spare seat for the deceased with her vase full of ashes sat on her plate, and the stories began from one seated guest to the next. Some were grand stories and others small, almost invisible. Some were funny and others downright sad. A toast was given with champagne for the mom to be and baby on the way. Kristan didn't tell the table about Pearl's baby, or the abortion, as it wasn't her place but she quietly toasted and nodded to the empty seat.

Jeremy took a picture of Kristan in her beautiful sundress standing at the table, adorned with endless flower arrangements from earlier in the day, and her small champagne flute filled with bubbles. He sent her a copy to her phone. He said you should send one to your mother, love Jeremy.

A few days later the autopsy report came from Pearl's doctor's office. Inside was a letter from her doctor. Miss Kristan, I write to you these words along with the autopsy report. You likely knew her whole medical condition as you watched it unfold since the beginning of the year. One can never fully know the ultimate cause as we are not God but we can surmise and this is what is meant by probable cause. She had an abortion, an incomplete one that caused inflammation of the uterine lining with bacteria held in her uterus. Antibiotics may have helped this if she had sought treatment. Her white count escalated but she thought she had the flu and several colds. One of these viruses laid the ultimate damage to her heart causing the cardiomyopathy. Her immune system was compromised and she was unable to fight off the viruses with ease. Essentially in all likelihood the abortion started this matter. Maybe even the injection given by the drug addict. Sadly. Remember one cannot be certain, and these procedures are done all the time without consequence, but unfortunately this may have precipitated her misfortune, coupled with the colds and flu. If you ever need to speak please feel free to call me. Elaine.

And just like that one may never know exactly. Medicine was not an exact science-she heard her mother say that over and over. But the hospital did save her life in between all this. And for that Kristan was grateful. She must bury this now. Her friend was gone, her friend who encouraged her, endlessly, was deceased. Answers and truth would come later. God would show her the way to that.

The next morning the phone rang and it was Kim from Atlanta. She was on her way. Was she ready for the road trip to celebrate Memorial Day weekend? She told her yes. She was prepared to begin a new life while leaving another behind.

Chapter 26). Memorial Weekend Holiday

The black suburban sure looked like an official government agency car thought Kristan. Her belongings fit in the back with room to spare. Good thing as she needed to go home for the summer after the trip to Destin. She hadn't planned that part out yet. Maybe her mom and dad would come pick her up, maybe Kim would drive back and drop her off. There was plenty of time to sort it all out. The most important thing for her would occur in a couple weeks but for the congresswoman the next three days were paramount. What would she find out? What was she looking for? Kristan and she had all the time in the world with a small adventure during it all. They were on a road trip with two diversions. This would help her ease her mind, in fact it would be a total distraction until Tuesday. Today was Friday and they would be there in about two hours. The couple of hours gave both of them a chance to get better acquainted. The small talk began and progressed to the two main topics.

Basically, Kim, who was trained in the military was doing some covert operation pertaining to some recent data mining incident. That's all Kristan needed to know. Some stories Kim would obtain would be highly personable and none of this would interfere with Kristan. She would be taking these interviews at an off location while Kristan rested at the farm. That seemed harmless she thought. The person in the back was also on the mission and acted as a bodyguard for both of them. Not so okay but whatever. Her life was topsy-turvy this first year and nothing, she supposed, could surprise her now.

"When we stop at a rest stop I will have you wear this eye covering-that way you don't know the location of the farm," she said.

"What about phones?" she asked.

"We will turn our location off and he'll keep our phones. We will use walkie-talkies to speak to one another until we have left the farm. You'll be in very reliable hands. Trust me. Your mother knows all this. I spoke with her."

"Secretive. Must definitely be important," Kristan surmised.

"Sometimes truths are hidden and we must find the light or the answers to someone's troubles," Kim said.

"Hope you find what you are looking for," Kristan responded.

"Evil exists. You're bright, you know that, right?"

"Yes. But I like to think it doesn't happen."

"Oh, I know. For the most part everything runs smoothly, until there's a breakdown just like a car. Then we have to help it to run again or find the problem and fix it."

Kristan liked that analogy. Fix the car, find the broken

part and replace it.

"You'll love the farm. It's quite beautiful. Managed perfectly. You may not even want to leave, I'm told."

"Looking forward to a few days away. Sounds nice."

"We'll be there for lunch."

They stopped at the rest stop and gave their phones to the bodyguard in the back seat, then Kristan took a nap with her eyes covered. This was the least of any problems. In fact she imagined she was at a spa with music playing and pleasurable scents surrounding her.

Kim looked at her bodyguard in the back seat and he gave a thumbs up. Everything had been planned about this meeting and now it was happening. She looked at her passenger and thought what a brave little soul she was. She seemed to be in a happy place with her decision and moved accordingly. The driver was also happy to be a part of this venture. She wanted to help young people-especially, young women. Having met one benefactor in Atlanta helped immensely. This woman was heaven sent and had much more to offer than she could. But she could help with her skills learned in the forces and others to assist. Almost divine one would say. Some things fall into place at the right time. She pulled in the long drive which led to the farmhouse. Surrounded by rows and rows of crops and foliage natural to the area the house was indeed hidden. The drive rounded with a curve to the right and then finally to the left ending with large trees and some pines nestled here and there. She circled around and stopped. Colorful flowers were everywhere of many types framing the house and paths leading away to the barn and other out buildings. She turned off the engine.

The car was completely emptied when Kristan finally woke up.

"We're here."

"Oh, I'm coming. Let me get my suitcase."

"It's all unloaded and in the house. Let's get you inside."

Kristan opened her door and stepped out. She looked ahead at the house with all the pretty flowers. Nice. She walked up with Kim to the door and out came a woman with long shiny caramel colored hair flowing down both sides of her face. Such a welcoming site.

"Hello dear, I'm Kate."

"I'm Kristan. A pleasure to meet you," she said.

"And me, too," she replied.

"You live here?"

"Me and many others. Please come in. We've made a special lunch for our new guests, that being you and Kim."

"Thank you." Kristan walked in from the covered front porch filled with ferns and soft porch furniture to a grand entrance of wood planked floors and runners separating two large front rooms. In the foyer was her luggage and other items.

"Don't worry about your luggage. Someone will take your bags upstairs to your room. Let's come back here and have some lunch."

Kristan could smell something but she wasn't sure what it was. Maybe it was bread, or dessert. She didn't know. But it smelled sweet, like honey. "Smells like honey," she said quietly.

"That's because it is. You have good senses Miss Kristan."

They continued walking to the back of the house where a large kitchen opened before them. It had floor to ceiling teal colored cabinets and a maple wood island set atop with white and over on a distant wall was a built in fireplace and windows open to the back where one could see the barn, gardens and a fire pit.

She began introducing Kristan to everyone seated at the table.

"Come and sit. Are you hungry?"

"Yes. It smells delicious."

"We made you a southern style lunch of BBQ, Brunswick Stew, cornbread and greens. You smelled the honey coming in as we warmed it on the stove top. Peach cobbler with vanilla yogurt is for dessert. We don't eat this fancy a lunch every day but it is a holiday so enjoy!"

The dishes were passed around and one lady served the stew to each person standing beside them. She smiled sweetly and seemed extremely happy.

"The cornbread has some jalapenos just so you know." Kate added.

Kristan filled her plate and ate. She drank sweet tea with lemons squeezed in as refreshment. There were flower petals on the table as adornment. Crossing her mind that she might need to reciprocate and make a meal, she thanked them again for this delicious lunch treat. "What can I do to help around here?"

"Don't worry about today. You can help tomorrow and this weekend. We are planning a cookout on Monday," Kate said.

Looking around the table sat a lady with a small child next to her. Her name was Maria and her daughter's name was Hope. She asked her her age and made some small talk with the child. Kim sat next to Kate and across from Kristan. Kim had been informed of the mother and child from her own sister's demise as Maria had been a victim that night at the marble place by the river. While an older light skinned black woman, dressed up more formal, quietly sat at the opposite end. A young gentleman of about age 20 sat next to her. The lady serving the stew sat next to the lady at the end. There were eight in all for lunch including Kristan. She enjoyed herself and tried to get to know their names. She assisted with the cleanup dreaming of a nap after she put her things away for the weekend. The body guard from the back seat brought her suitcases upstairs and Kate showed them her room. The view ensconced the large poster bed adorned with comfortable pillows. She could see two more young men out near the barn. She wondered how many people lived here.

"How many people live here Kate?"

"There's around twelve people here at any one time with some coming and going."

"Oh, I see," she replied.

"We are building another bunk house for four more guests but that won't be ready until next year. I'll fill you in tomorrow at breakfast of what we do. Breakfast is at eight and dinner tonight is lunch leftovers. We'll be doing much more cooking over the weekend. Please be comfortable."

"I'm going to take a short nap, if you don't mind."

"Not at all, see you when you rise."

Chapter 27). Breakfast at Eight

Kristan woke, showered, dressed (informally), and made way for the kitchen. She was always hungry now and growing. Her belly was definitely growing, she could feel it stretching, sometimes, overnight. She glanced in the hallway mirror. She looked rather wonderful, motherly, like from the Bible or something. Some would call this the maternal glow.

"Look at you!" Kate fussed over her as she walked into the large kitchen. "You're glowing."

"Do you think so?"

"Don't think. I know it. It's that gush of blood and nutrients filling that baby, making it ready to come out in a couple weeks. Is it dancing inside there?"

"Yes, all the time. But I don't mind because it's alive and that brings me joy."

"Well little missy. This is what's happening and what you need to know for the day. There's a schedule. That's how we operate. Your partner, Miss Kim, has already high tailed it to the swamp," Kate said with pleasure.

"She's gone?'

"Oh yeah. In the skiff by sunup, then into a canoe, followed by a short walk deep into the Okefenokee. Her and the gentleman will be at an outpost all day, then sleep in an old swamp house near a dock at night and gone all day tomorrow. We will see them either Sunday night or Monday morning, depending."

"Depending? On what?" Kristan was aroused with curiosity. She had much to learn here on the farm and what really happens in the swamp.

"No bother right now. We'll get to the swamp talk tonight by the fire out back. That makes for great storytelling. Here's the schedule, the meals, the work to be done, of which you are excused from being two weeks away from delivery."

"I can cook and clean the kitchen," she said wanting to feel useful.

"I thought you might say that. You do lunch today, it's for twelve. Two left and two are arriving, so that makes twelve. Today is grilled bacon, cheese, and tomato sandwiches with a salad from the garden topped with our homemade dressing. Lemonade with raspberries followed by cherry pie, low sugar crust, with almond ice cream. Maria and Hope will help you in the kitchen at eleven o'clock. Hope is learning to set the table."

"Sounds like a plan. Thank you."

"Let's go into the front room and I'll tell you all about our farm."

Kristan followed Kate into the front room which was half office and half old time salon, or a waiting room. Large windows let in the light of the day or closed it off nestling togetherness and confidences. This morning it was set for the confidence of three persons: Kate the instructor, Kristan the student, and Sara the benefactor who happens to sing opera. Kristan would find this out later this afternoon in the room opposite from where they sat. So much to learn. Enjoy. She told herself. She was loving the distraction from herself. Except the glow. She kept glowing and Sara noticed. Because nothing escaped her vision.

The three of them sat sipping coffee and tea. On the side were cheddar wafers with an almond on top. Kristan had never seen these before. Her mother had been to Paris, lived there, so they occasionally had very French food or delicacies from other lands. But this cute little button had escaped her palate and it was tasty. She ate a few more.

"We make those Kristan. Do you like?" said Sara.

"Scrumptious. It just tastes good with my tea," she added.

"We are going to be selling them. I'm opening an online store for several products. Working on that right now. The money will benefit The Palmetto Stars Plantation."

"Love that name. How did that come to be?" asked Kristan.

"At night, there's stars and stars, and sometimes you see a palmetto. Both natural, both cutting. Actually, a relative of mine ran into one one night and ended up seeing stars. That's a fireside tale." Sara sat there smiling. Guess there's more to that story. No worries.

"Onto business. Kristan, here is the farm's philosophy and what we do here. It's not long. Have a read and then we'll tell you more."

Kristan read the page in the book explaining the plantation, how it started, and what it hopes to accomplish. Written by Sara Callais. "It's you, you're the owner."

"Yup, it's my place. But actually it belongs to everyone that comes here. We work together to make it a unique place, or haven for who it inspires."

Kate said, "Kristan, we wanted you to know about this place because James is our friend. You haven't met him yet but we understand he is going to be the father, he and Megan will be the parents of your baby to be."

"Yes. I hear they are a fine couple and have three boys already. I have spoken on the phone with them and we have Face Timed."

"We hope you will visit us again in the future and not be a stranger. Your child will likely visit here from time to time. This can be a connection, as well as the parents."

"Thank you. That's sweet. I'll remember that."

Sara rose and stood there quietly, then said, "Kristan,

you and I can have an hour together later this afternoon. I'd like to play the piano for you and sing a song or two."

"I would love that. What time?"

"How about five o'clock."

She smiled and left the room. Kate started informing her of who was coming today and who was here and why. She explained the treatments which they had endured for cancer, and their recovery here. "Some are sicker than others, some have left hope behind when doctors can do no more. Some of our care for them is palliative but we have seen miracles, too. Others have been in foster care for too long with no place to go. Several of the boys here are from that situation. The hard work of farming uses their energy and brings them peace. No one is a felon but a few were on their way. We hope we impact their life and they never return. If they do something above our allowances, they are gone immediately and we have just a few at a time. This way they can work together, encourage one another, etc. The cancer patients also encourage one another and much of the day is centered away from their condition as they forget about it and begin to heal. I'm not telling you we are faith healers, gypsies, or anything of the kind. We give love, appreciation, the right foods five days a week as weekends are mini splurges. All in all we motivate, spread positivity and support one another. It works. It really does. If someone seems stressed we send them on an exercise trip." She laughed.

"I don't know what to say," said Kristan. She'd known people with cancer and they seem to whittle away to nothing after the severe chemotherapy. Many seemed to survive her mother always said but for the ones who didn't make it-it was devastating for their families and obviously the patient. "I'd like to see one of these who made it after a poor prognosis."

"You will tonight. In fact you already saw her. She was serving the Brunswick stew yesterday. She can show you her pictures tonight. She looked like a drug addict two years ago, tragically thin, wrinkled and told to go home and die peacefully. She contemplated that and became aware of our place down here in southern Georgia. You must have a referral. Miss Sara doesn't want fakers or journalists pretending. She wants real people who are sick with nowhere to go. She tells me after ten years with results then we'll invite in the journalist. First we must try, be honest and see if we are onto something."

"Thank you for your honesty. As if there's nothing left to lose, the last hope. Don't give up the ship attitude."

"I once read about a man who had lung cancer and the doctor told him it was incurable. He could not operate or do anything. So the man left, and went back to his garden, his life, and didn't tell anyone and had no treatments. One day down the road the man goes back to the doctor and says, 'I didn't die like you said I would.' The doctor was shocked. His life had been restored and the cancer was completely gone. It happened."

"You mean miracles happens. Wow, quite a story. It's actually a hopeful story to not believe everything someone tells you in life."

"See even you are a positive outlook for your own future."

She smiled. She looked around. She liked this whole idea. She was sure her mother would too. The thought crossed her mind that she might even see her child here or in Destin someday. She'd get to interact and say hello. That would be good for both of them. Mostly, though, she'd let the parents be parents and the kid would know but she wouldn't interfere. Could it really be this pleasant she wondered? This place would tell you yes. Yes. Yes.

"We are working on spices, eliminating fertilizers, mind body techniques, fasting periodically, and immune boosters. We do speak with immunologists about certain cell factors in turning on and off these proteins. Also the brain is the mystery being discovered. I'd say it's a brain-heart thing myself. The two seem so connected through our neurological system. It's what makes us tick." Kate explained.

"I had hoped to enter a nursing program but this makes me excited. Maybe I should look into being a physician's assistant or an MD. But that's a lifetime and lots of money. Not sure it's worth it," Kristan elongated her state of mind about school.

"Maybe you will find something different. One thing at a

time. First your three days here to relax, then a small trip, finally the baby and home you go to your mother."

Hope and Maria appeared in the hallway outside the office, or salon. "I'm in here ladies. Time to make the lunch?"

"Yes, we are ready," said Maria. Kristan excused herself and walked with the mother and daughter to the kitchen. She was ready to be of service.

Chapter 28). The Swamp

Eric, the bodyguard from the backseat was Kim's partner for the two day swamp excursion. Eric had extensive training in the Special Forces. Hence, that's why he was here with her for this journey. The two of them would capitulate to the area and meet with victims followed by an unidentified whistleblower. Identifications would not be offered up on either side, only to a third party who made these meetings available. The goal ... to obtain the truth, seek justice through the proper agency and prepare to make laws that would negate this behavior.

Kim wasn't thinking about the meetings she was looking at all the swamp land around her. They were met by a small boat captain at a dock close to the Okefenokee Swamp border at 6:30 am. He had a Carolina Skiff boat made in nearby Waycross, Georgia. The water was up and plenty of it to fill the lake and rivers surrounding the swamp. He'd take them to Perch Lake where they'd get their canoe and paddle down river to the ultimate lake, Half Moon Lake. They should make it to Half Moon before 11 am and secure their path to the old swamp house. From there they'd travel a shorter distance to the "Shack."

Captain Earl started off his regular routine as he jaunted over smooth seas this morning without a current or a wave. "Thanks for joining me folks. You are in for an experience today and before you get to do that, well, it's my job to inform you about the place. The Okefenokee is 600 square miles and not like the ocean when you get lost, but as difficult to find because of the critters which inhabit these waters and shores."

Captain Earl tipped his hat, swept it over the swamp to the shore and back again for intense meaning and to get his passengers attention. He stalled the boat and put it into neutral, furthering his charade. "These 700 square miles of refuge lying mostly in Georgia contain ten thousand alligators, mostly in the southern portion in 2-10 feet of water. There's water moccasins, Black Bear, otter, tortoises, osprey, cranes, white tailed deer, and bobcats in this 7,000 year old swamp. It forms the Suwanee River which is contained in the Coastal Plain and is 250 miles from Atlanta. The trees though make it unique. We have giant tupelo and bald cypress with the champagne of honey coming from the tupelo. The mild vanilla nectar is a buttery sweet flavor. The bees make it best but the tree is famous from Van Morrison singing about his wife. There's a farm not far from here that makes it. She sells it online and to restaurants. Well, I believe that all you need to know from me. First aid sites are out there-look at your map. These sites have phones that call in foul play such as an animal bite, snake or gator attack. Be alert. No open food. Any questions?"

Eric and Kim looked at each other. He had a registered gun but would use it to scare anything away. Kim planned on staying right next to him for the next 36-48 hours. Absolutely right next to him. She'd been trained as well but alligators, bears and, yes, snakes were not on her list of bedtime Lovie's. They each gave a thumbs up.

"No questions. Okay. Bring the canoes back to this post, I'll pick you up Sunday night at 6 pm or Monday morning at 7 am. Sharp. No waiting." He sped the boat up and crossed over to a dock. He slowed. He tied up. They got off and transferred their equipment to the dock. He pointed to the canoes. Eric went and eased the canoe into the water and loaded the middle with their belongings which were light. Earl handed them two life jackets as per policy. He untied his boat, put the boat in reverse and pulled away. He waved as he sped away. They were set with map, compass, walkie talkies and food supplies, not to mention water, paper, pen, and cell phones for video and recording purposes.

Chapter 29). The Swamp

Kim paddled from the front and Eric sat back to steer from either side of the canoe. They canoed slowly meandering quietly.

"Listen, do you hear that?" she asked.

"No, I don't hear anything," he replied.

Nothing was moving. All was still. Kim looked up to see if any birds were in the blue sky. The sun had been up for two hours. Nothing. Then she looked over to the right edge of the lake they would be leaving soon. Foliage, small trees, and muck everywhere inhibited her view until she saw one, then another. She was initially afraid to move another muscle or speak. Instead she pointed with her paddle that was already out of the water. She stopped breathing, holding her breath until she could paddle again. Her muscles clamped up and became taut. Her sense told her to fly up out of here and get away from danger. Behind her she heard him say, "There's five drying themselves off, getting a suntan, waiting to leap into action."

"What the fuck?" she mumbled.

Her skin flushed and she took a deep breath. All right, shake it off, not going to be afraid of fucking alligators. She put her paddle in the water, watching the five flesh eating reptile's poolside, and released a slow smooth full depth scoop to propel them forward.

"I can't look back. What are they doing?"

"They are swimming towards us, paddle faster," he said quickly.

"What? No way!"

"Don't look now but one is beside us," he said.

"I know you're kidding me, right?"

She took a quick look when her paddle came up out of the water behind her. Truth. There it was swimming beside them.

A few birds flew overhead. She wished that's all it was. Then her partner sitting behind her said, "We are going to go left and lose this guy. He looks hungry."

"You can't tell that," she answered.

"No but I think he sees your bright colored shirt and you are just his size. I've got my gun to scare him if need be. Believe me, partner, you come first. Ten thousand alligators in here, they won't miss one."

"Likely, it's illegal to kill one," she said.

"Not when its hunting season, or your life is in danger," he said.

Quickly he maneuvered the canoe to head left, go fast and then corrected back to the middle of the lake. They would be over this lake soon and onto the meandering river connecting it to their destination. Tall trees emerged as they entered deeper into the swamp. It held large lower trunks, these just didn't exist anywhere else. How did they live in the water without getting waterlogged or rotten? He needed to read up on that. He couldn't understand it. But he did suppose they adapted over time, a long time ago.

Gliding into the waterway the edges of shore came closer together. She wondered what they might see back here. Maybe some otter or even a black bear. It was then she told herself to look for fish.

"Tell me, Kim, why did you get into this here assignment?"

"Long story," was her quick reply.

"Tell me the story, then we'll be there."

"I knew I didn't want to fly planes and being on a ship was too confining. Killing folks and blowing them to pieces didn't interest me but I respect what they do for us. Working in an office only at the computer seemed too secretary-ish. I chose special forces with intelligence using my people skills and stay alive skills combined."

"Except alligators scare you," he reminded her.

"They are man eating reptiles and this is a preserve, so I can't kill them but they can kill me. No sense."

"Any other animals frighten you?"

"Bears," she said quietly.

"Bears," he screamed.

"And snakes," she added.

"You hit the jackpot, missy," he laughed.

"That's why you're here. You are the excellent marksman, outdoorsman and king of the sharpshooters, so I'm in good hands."

"They did say ... you are guarding the Queen so be alert."

"I was born a Queen," she smirked.

"Okay, you got me."

She turned and looked at her partner. Laughed out loud. Pointed at herself, "My name means Queen. Born that way."

"Well, I hope the Queen gets all her answers later today. We should be hitting the other lake in about an hour."

Kim paddled on and on. She saw fish, ducks, birds, pretty trees, flowers and a blue sky.

The two paddled up to the dock in Half Moon Lake, Eric grabbed hold while Kim fixed the line on the cleat. They were careful not to rock the canoe and tip it over. Eric lifted and put their belongings on the dock. They left it in the water as they'd be canoeing a couple times over the next day or two. Behind the dock was a screen enclosure for all the swamp goers to sit inside from the habitat, read a map, and purchase a water or snack. It even had an emergency call phone and sitting beside that was a defibrillator. Like out here someone is going to need that. Not sure they could get to them in time. Then again, maybe if one had a heart attack or arrhythmia being scared from a bear, snake, or alligator they could be helped. Surely Kim was in good health and young, a defibrillator would not be needed.

They sat inside away from the sun which was directly overhead now. Once they cooled off from some water it was time for the next trek. Into the woods to the swamp house or shack where the two girls had been brought in by the secret service and the whistleblower. Yes, this was a military operation with secrecy. Each knew as much as they were to know. Everyone did not know everything, except her. This would be her last operation and then back to being a congresswoman elect. Her future looked bright, that's what they told her. She'd evaluate it. She wanted to tell her partner Eric that her main goal was to help women and girls achieve more in life from all avenues.

"I got in to help women and children," she stated matter-of-factly.

He looked at her. That was a nice thing to say. Where did that come from he thought?

She could tell he was evaluating her statement. "It comes from my mom being all alone in the world with two kids and no husband. It made a lasting impression." She surprised herself with her thoughts expressed aloud.

"You got a good soul, Miss Kim."

"Yeah."

"Now let's get to work," he commanded.

They followed the trail for two miles to the shack which wasn't a shack but an old, very old, wooden house with two stories. Kim thought to herself the place appeared old and dry, and where was the fire department if it goes up in smoke. She guessed pails and pails of water from an outside well would work. One night and two days. This seemed extreme on the inside but to another it looked normal visiting the Okefenokee Swamp, something someone does all the time. She laughed.

"The absurdity, right?"

"You can read me that well?"

"Someday, you'll be as good as me," he said and laughed.

"How absurd can you be?"

They were actually enjoying this venture. Let's look

inside he thought.

He stepped inside and the place was different-it looked newer, cozy and livable. This will work. He heard a noise upstairs and he stopped walking.

"Listen."

Footsteps came towards the top of the stairs and an old man appeared. He waved.

"I been waitin, glad you here. Use da kitchen, drinks in da fridge." Then he disappeared.

"I can follow orders. Can you?"

Into the kitchen they went and set up the phone recorder and video. Ready. Kim pulled out her notebook. She wasn't allowed to take notes she could only scratch words that prompted her questions. This was all about the victims.

Eric grabbed two cokes from the fully stocked fridge. He closed it and it creaked loudly which sent shivers up Kim's spine. She rolled her own eyes at herself. Her partner just laughed lightly. She smiled back. On with it. Let's roll.

The first woman came down completely covered with a robe and veil. The old man led her to the table and left. She lifted the veil for Kim to see her face, then she was fingerprinted and covered her face once again. Kim asked her if she would like a drink and she said yes.

"Here you go. I'm so sorry you have to go through this. I hope it doesn't hurt or bring up too many memories which are upsetting," Kim said.

"Thank you. I appreciate the sentiment. I don't know where to begin."

"Just start at the beginning and go forth. If something is a theory-that's okay, too. Sometimes what our gut tells us is a way of exposing the truth. When it's a thought, then just add that, that it is a thought, not a fact."

"Sounds good."

Chapter 30). Swamp Shack

"My name is Martha and I suppose this is an internet story. I got online to protect my kids. We didn't grow up with the internet, or phones, and I would hear stories all about how scary it was. I joined social Medias and friended people I knew. I blogged, etc. I had just had a major surgery which I didn't broadcast to anyone but somehow it seemed others knew my business. At one point, I felt, can't put my finger on it, like someone was waterboarding me, psychologically. I remember thinking they asked me something, then made a statement how extreme my idea was. It was as though they were goading me along. I thought, this must be the way the internet is, right?! I suppose I may have been stalked, or something. Maybe my computer was hacked. One time foreign writing came across the blog I was on, like there was a person inside the computer writing on it. Totally weird. Someone was definitely more advanced than me. Why did I stay on the internet? Some would ask. Because I wanted to write a book. I always have wanted to write a book since I was in my twenties. I tried to learn through blogging and for a while it seemed some people were trying to help me. It was a positive thing until it wasn't. My sister kept encouraging me to get on all the social Medias. Have you tried this or that, etc.? I wrote my first novel and asked her to edit the English, punctuation, etc. She wouldn't. I was crushed. What now? I then wrote another novel, a full length novel, feeling like I could do it. It was in a place I'd never been to or seen. I have always wanted to go there-so

I wrote about Paris. I even had coffee with a writer mother whom I met on social media and she was writing a book too. We had a lovely time. Then I began my first full length novel. I traveled around virtually and needed a plot so I added the hunger and starvation in Africa, especially during the droughts which cause famines that I'd seen on the news. Terrible. I kept learning, I kept writing. The first book I wrote was a little steamy (Fifty Shades of Gray was out and everyone was reading it). Remember I didn't know about ratings, except for movies. Then I changed it to a middle grade novel and made it all about coming of age, family style, globally. It turned into a real beautiful novel, three books actually. During the middle of it something happened, and someone really came after me. The social media sites I surmised or guessed was cops or FBI placed pictures on there that I still can't get out of my mind. It was awful. I didn't know what to do. I thought they were going to come to my house and arrest me for child porn or something. I didn't ask for it. I didn't go to a new place looking for it. It just appeared. I was stunned. I reported it to the social media site. It looked like a young girl having hard core sex with a man in his twenties or older and I was beside myself. It was not a child but maybe a teen like seventeen. I really felt someone was after me. How could this happen? It was disgusting. Then another picture came on and it was an older woman and she was tied up, legs spread apart and held with leather in an awful position. Once again someone either hacked or purposefully showed me these photos. It was not like the Fifty Shades of Gray with the whole mommy porn, where its play acting, and everyone is safe. This picture looked torturous. I felt betrayed by some people I followed, the blogs, all of it. I still can't get those photos out of my mind. Never in a million years would I want to see torture put upon women or children. That's just not me. But the fact they had lured me there to be on social media and make blogs, write poetry, write a novel, be active and engage with others. I learned to make a GIF, a post, write a 500 word journalistic type post or article, and make comments. Be an artist. The fact that someone could get to me or frame me frightened me. That's why I think it was hacked by authorities going over and above who I was really following. Which is rather frightening if someone can come on your phone or cable network and pretend to be someone else. What else can they do? Shut your business down? Follow you and terrorize you? I call these people terrorists. I became afraid for my life. Thinking what wouldn't they do? They also showed pictures of movies my brother was in as he had a history of writing and acting as an extra. He sued some people, so I thought, what do they want with me? Once on vacation in the summer of 2014, after all these incidents on the net, a security guard asked me what I was reading on the beach. He stopped and talked with me a long, long time. When we had arrived the car next to ours was the vehicle I used in my big novel with a placard using my last name, my maiden name. I didn't see this as a coincidence. This was to hurt me, scare me and maybe warn me like I'm watching you. I didn't really put all this together until I went back and it fell into place. The episodes were connected to hurt me. Back in 2013 I told my family that I thought the FBI was after me. I told them about the issues I was having with the internet. My mother had invited them in to sit at her kitchen table and discuss my brother's case with them. I saw them. I didn't sit with them. This was around 2012-2013. She thought they would help her, that's what they told her. He wanted justice but justice had six ways to Sunday and they gave him until Sunday, then crushed him every step of the way. I believe in our law enforcement, lady justice, the American way, but for a while I was screaming inside that they were looking to frame me. I have a great life, had a great career and never have I had any trouble. Whatsoever. I suddenly felt for the framed person from anything, drugs, or whatever. Very hard to prove yourself if they want you and they wanted my brother real bad. I prayed for him. For a while after my big surgery I thought maybe someone was trying to help me through poetry, art and kindness. One of my patients told me about this kind of program in psychology. Art Therapy. Made sense. Her own daughter was enrolled. She said they had it at the college she worked for. But I didn't need therapy. I was let go, fired, from my job in January 2015 because they came in and deleted positions, cut salaries, sent the CEO to another hospital to manage and gave him a $4 million dollar a year position. Companies do that, celebrate the upper circles and fire the worker, the nurses, lab and others. The summer before around September my coworker who was in charge of the place who had hired me had my neighbors name on her calendar for a meeting. She did work for a major New York firm. I thought that so strange. Maybe I was going a little mad, not really, because eventually pieces of the puzzle fit together and made a picture of truth. Anyway the internet became my friend again in 2015-2016. I found other writers but I never trusted again. I was just waiting for someone to take me down again. It's horrible and the only thing I can think of is internet terrorism. I was terrified. I was scared. I was afraid. And I got on to protect my children. If I couldn't protect myself what will happen to our children? The feeling I eventually had, not at the time, was that computer hackers or FBI agents put a trace on my phone and pretended to be the very person who I was following interrupting real truth and exchanges. Both of my phones, I believe, had been hacked. Then looking back I know who they were, at least pretending to be. It wasn't until I saw a movie where police can turn on your camera from a distance. How creepy. How intrusive. Once at a nursing class she had my phone by herself and asked me to come to lunch with her. I think she taped me. God I know I sound like psychotic or lunatic, but because of my brother, I thought it real. Several times my phone turned on, all by itself, that is the video camera and I didn't do it. Once when I was in the bathtub and several times at my kitchen counter. Psychological waterboarding and Internet Terrorism could only be done by bad actors, someone trained in these tactics of gut punching another. Something you'd see in an old Chinese movie or war movie. It did cross my mind maybe nefarious hackers (foreign countries if you watch the news) did it. Several times while watching the news I said I already know that, I know they do that because it's been done to me. The phone companies were always out with their trucks on our street. They had many issues for several years trying to put in lines. It was a new neighborhood. Or maybe police did it, maybe they do that to people on social media sites looking for bad people. Finally, I read a book in January 2020 and in reading it I thought that's what happened to me. I felt like I lived in that book. This was written by a Pulitzer Prize Writer.

I just want you to know it still affects me today because I don't know exactly what happened, just that I lived it, and it shouldn't happen to anyone else, ever. I was reminded when the President said if they can do it to me, they can do it to you. I said to myself they did it to me back in 2012-2014 when I got on social media and after a major surgery. There's Hippa Laws and I think someone is guilty of a violation of stealing medical privacy and threatening the psychological health of an individual."

"Is that everything?"

"No. I have so much more to expand on, more incidents. But I need a break."

"Okay, let's break."

Chapter 31). Murder for Mary; Martha Returns

Mary was brought down as Martha rested to collect her thoughts and be brave again. Mary was a black woman and covered up like Martha. The same procedure was done, one facial look, fingers printed and a one way conversation of her truths.

Eric figured out that Kim was handling these women with kid's gloves to extract more information and tie it in with the whistleblower who would be speaking last. Secrecy was paramount and truth mattered, even though media seemed to be one sided. True government has to be held accountable for ALL the people. Bad marbles had to be let go from the game, pure and simple, because our own security needed to be close to perfect as possible. She was trusted but also looked over from above. She liked the responsibility. She'd always held responsible positions and felt compelled to do the right thing. Eric listened. This case was more difficult.

"State your name and begin with your recollection, even through your medical condition."

"My name is Mary. I'm here to represent my dead sister Laura. She was in a difficult marriage and found herself pregnant. She gave birth to a stillborn child. It was traumatic. I was heartbroken for her and not prepared for what was to come. Her husband and she began fighting and they had never done that before. He had been elusive, and possibly, not forthcoming on his business trips. One night she was reading her phone and a text told her where the gun was hidden in her home. Why did this person want her to know this?"

"She found the gun and when she went back to read the text, as if someone was going to tell her what to do with it, she called me all about this episode. I don't know what I was thinking. I fell asleep. She hadn't been eating. She had headaches. Her condition coupled with this person texting confused her. Her vision was blurred when she woke up. She told me she looked around and did not know where she was. I walked around it was still the middle of the night and wondered if I needed to go over and help her adjust. Then she received another text. It said bring the gun and meet this person at the parking lot for the federal building in the morning. I have no idea except maybe this person was watching her or listening to her. She was very distraught. She didn't tell me this part about the gun. Next thing she did was go to the federal building and drove around looking for a place to park. You can see her on video camera searching the parking lot or looking for a person. She had the gun right next to her. She would never use it, doesn't really know how to. She pulled in one space but pulled out and then tried to park in another space. Some security guard or policeman came at her and she was confused. They radioed for help and more came around citing a deranged lady who was driving erratically near federal property. What was she doing? So she tried to park again, and he looked in through her window, saw the gun and started calling on his radio again for back up. Then he pointed his gun at her. Still confused and not seeing who she was supposed to meet she drove quickly and they fired the gun into her car killing her. And here I am. Strange. I don't know what to make of it. Police had her phone and none of the texts or our call were found. It appears to have been wiped clean of any disturbances she received. I know she was experiencing postpartum depression but someone wanted her dead. Possibly. Why do I say this? Because her husband has a girlfriend and new life. He has connections that go a bit deep. Oh, and yeah I took a picture of that screenshot she sent because the gun thing was something Laura would never do. She didn't even like to touch them. After I secured it on my son's phone I erased it from my phone. I'm not even sure why I did that. But I did. And I have it with me. I'm better now. But I hope you can find out what happened. I don't want people to get away with murder even if they forced it upon her. Maybe the security guard was in on it with the husband. I know I sound farfetched but it seemed like the police didn't really satisfy me with their investigation, maybe because it was one of their own. She had postpartum depression, even post-delivery psychosis, maybe. I don't know if it was a prank or someone wanted her to hurt someone or get herself killed. I hope you find something. I think it was a hacker or ex policeman, someone who knew how to intrude and make her look more lunatic than she was. Maybe they got a payment from the life insurance money."

"Thank you for telling me your story. And I'm glad you are all right. I'm very sorry about your sister and her baby.

It does seem needless, like why go to lengths of meeting someone with a gun?"

"Thank you. I'm glad someone is looking into these internet cybercrimes. It's like the invisible monster is no longer under the bed but everywhere a phone transmits."

"That's a remarkable way of putting it." Kim held her hands.

She returned upstairs and the elder gentleman appeared at the top. "We have an extra person but we feel it's important and that you'd want hear his story. We just found him."

"Please send him down."

Another covered up individual came down. He knew the drill. Show his face, fingerprinted and never talk about this interview ever again unless in a closed court case.

"Brian, I'm glad to talk with you."

"Thanks."

"Just start at the beginning and explain."

"My boyfriend and I had been dating about four months and he was on medication for depression. The doctors decided to switch it and that's when he really went downhill. I believe it was the new medication. I looked it up and the consequences are dire. I went to a black market sight on the internet where you can find out what others are prescribed."

"Seriously, there is a sight like that?"

"On the black web. Yes."

"Continue."

"I asked around and found out that he was taking the same medication as a few other famous people had taken prior to their suicides. I thought what is going on? This medication must be bad or everyone is getting very sick at the same time."

"Sounds conspiratorial."

"I know. But the person I reported this to thought someone should know. They brought me to you. Medicine can be very powerful making our thoughts and body processes act differently. Sometimes a blessing and maybe other times not so."

"You should not return to the sight online. However, I will need the address if you have it. I will seriously look into this information and I appreciate your search. And I'm saddened by your loss."

"I just thought four deaths by suicide with neck ties to a doorknob in three months and all using the same medicine seemed like bad medicine."

"We will check the lot and sales from which companies. Maybe I'll be able to obtain an analysis of the actual drug.

Do you still have the bottle?"

"I do and I brought it with me. Thanks for thinking I'm not an idiot. I mourned him and I'm okay. It just bugged me when I read about the others."

"Remember, no words to others. That is how this works. That's why I can't take everyone's case."

"I applaud you."

"Someone will visit you with any news about this. We will be thorough but no promises, one way or the other."

He reached out and held her hand. He gave it a slight squeeze and then stood up. He handed over his friend and lover's vial of pills. Then he returned to the upstairs gentleman. He would not be staying for dinner.

Eric and Kim pulled some chips out of the cupboard and sat at the kitchen table. The old man upstairs, estimated to be about 84 years old, said to get anything they wanted. It was on the house. He'd cook dinner later for all five of them.

"Do you have a name for this operation?" he asked.

"Yes. I named it after my sister, Rebekah. She was a fiery red head who died a few years ago after she got hooked on drugs and became jealous of her boyfriend's ex-girlfriends. She lost it. She was messed up. Tragically, she killed a girl, drugged another, and then was shot before she was able to plunge a sword into an innocent lady trying to help the situation."

"Wow."

"Yeah."

"That's some serious shit. I'm sorry about her."

"Rebekah's Storm, that's the name. Soon to be over. Finished. I'm out."

"But how will you help those in need?"

"I'm getting a team, a cybercrime team for surveillance and espionage that will work separate from the big agencies. Kind of like a watchdog for the watchdogs."

"Best on that. I think I hear her coming back down."

Martha sat down, showed her face, covered back up, finger printed again and began.

"Let me fill in a few more blanks, the weirdness of it all. Yes, I'm a sensitive person but some things just don't add up. The lady I had coffee with totally dismissed me a couple years later. We were at the same book fair showcasing our novels. She completely ignored me, would not even look at me. We were literally 12 inches from each other. I couldn't figure that one out. When I would ask her a question she wouldn't even look at me. Rude.

Finally, when I was leaving for the day she looked up at me from her chair and smiled a very small smile. Go figure. There's a story right there, I'd say. After I'd seen the two guys out front of my home playing with TV lines, and two women six years apart both near my phone I thought they are tracing me, using whatever gadgets they have sent to spy on me. But why? When you think someone is spying on you and you don't know if it's the good guys or the bad guys it freaks you out. It always came back to my brother who spent five years in a federal pen for something which later got lifted. Tell me how that works because I don't know? I am not his advocate but I think the whole family was watched and recorded. I should have been off limits, my husband and I both had a major surgery and were stressed from that. They completely went bonkers on me. I want to stand up for myself and I don't want others to get caught in the dragnet of the NSA and pick and choose who to bother. That's not American. There were men following me in stores, cops listening to my phone, showing up at a daughter's friend's party in another city busting into a party which wasn't even loud. They roughed up a few under age people that were with their older sister and brother. Climbing on top of them and putting their face to the ground a fifteen year old boy doing nothing but hiding behind a door. He was told this is what it feels like to be molested. Totally inappropriate. Following my other daughter and me out of a city on a quiet road for miles and miles. That's how they knew the other daughter was at a party because she texted me. This is big brother spying. This is 1984. Another guy was at a drugstore and was looking out a window when I saw him he ducked out of view. With parenting, marriage and writing books it became a bit stressful with that added unknown. My first three novels practically wrote themselves. I would say a six year period was extremely stressful with the phone and the brother thing. My brother got out and things quieted down for me. But my mother was very worried all the time. The TV would turn on or off by itself. A loud noise shook my older sister and me and the whole family became stressed by the incarceration. I tell people to watch out for what they say on social media, that you can get five years in the slammer if you say something harmful but celebrities and others do it all the time and no one goes to jail, only the private citizens for which somebody of power has something against you. The feeling I got was that things started out okay and dove deeper into craziness or maybe they wanted a family member all the time to make mistakes to get at them, is it AI, or the law, or bad actors? I was targeted maliciously with intent to harm. Two recent items I haven't figured out yet. I cut the hair of a lady detective because I saw her on a TV Documentary. She seemed real nice. Probably nothing. But the other item is deeply disturbing. I was living at an apartment complex for six months or so and this guy moved in with wild blonde hair, tall and started drilling in the walls, etc. He was walking outside talking on the phone like he wanted to be loud and obnoxious, so people would hear him. Weird. I moved. A few months later this guy hits my radar. I see someone across the river from where we are sitting enjoying a picnic during a holiday and he's walking along the river acting wildly, like attention getting. I look and he stares at me with this crazed look. I blink and try to think where I have seen him? I forget about it. I come home and receive some tragic news that I cannot comprehend yet. It doesn't add up. Maybe there are weirdos everywhere. I don't know. When I got home the day after Labor Day a distant family member had committed suicide on National Suicide Prevention Day and Month. I didn't know them but how tragic for a young life. I hope you can help people with your task force. Thank you for listening. Be Safe. Be Best."

"I almost forgot. This is real life, not phones. My sister and I went for coffee in a small hometown area and parked by the lighthouse. A car pulled up next to us and a guy sat there like us. Weird. But okay don't want to alarm my sister. I turn and take a quick picture of my sister and lo and behold the guy in the car squats down so you can't see his head. I take a deep breath. I'm just getting fucking coffee and sitting with my sister. When you feel like you're in the movie it's disheartening, invasive and extremely scary. An hour later we go for more coffee in the town next to ours where we both were born. We get the coffee and return to our car, which I had rented, and lo and behold there's another car with a black gentleman inside, window down smoking a cigarette parked right next to ours. I walked behind him and I wanted to go to the window and make small talk but I was furious. What the hell? Where's Colombo when you need him. My sister could not believe it and she became scared. She believed my observations to be correct. But why? Another time I went to buy a larger car at a dealership. I picked one out and went for a test drive. I told the seller I pretty much wanted it. I came back the next day and it was gone. Now who does that? And why would they let a car be transferred if it was going to be sold? Later on I figured that they were listening in on my car so they didn't want to bug another car. Much easier to not let her buy one. I know tell me I'm insane, right. But our hatchback never worked right like it was supposed to. I think my parents had it much worse and it affected my mother tremendously in a terrible way. The US Marshalls or forces came twice to her house in early morning raids with guns drawn. Tell me it takes seven trained guys to take down an 87 and 91 year old in their jammies to take into custody their 53 year old son who's never harmed anyone? But that is his story to tell-not mine. Just letting you know how we were affected as a family."

"You have given me quite a bit with dates and descriptions, feelings included too. I am going to put this against a whistleblower and from that we can check records and make a case. I'm going to work very hard. Thanks." Kim shakes her hand. "Go get some rest before dinner tonight."

Chapter 32). Sunday Night Campfire at Palmetto Stars Plantation

The Sunday night campfire at Palmetto Stars Plantation began around 4 PM setting up chairs around the outside fire pit. Around three o'clock Kristan showered and took a quick nap. Kate had promised to show her more of the outside today from the barn to the fields and beyond. She said she take her on a slow ATV over paths so she could see the place. The food was already prepped before noon allowing the afternoon and evening stress free. Kristan wore her Mother's Day slash funeral dress and felt very happy today. Something about this place that the more days you stayed the freerer you felt. Was it the land? Or the hostess? Maybe it was the whole group even though she didn't know anyone.

She laid down on her bed and fell asleep for forty five minutes. It was quiet this afternoon, sunny and beautiful. Flowers were in full bloom, everything else was bright green from the spring growth. She showered and dressed putting on flat cushioned sandals, something she would wear at a beach vacation, threw on a necklace and sprayed a dash of perfume. All set she walked down the stairway to meet up with Kate for a big tour.

"I'm out here on the golf cart."

"Coming."

"I thought we'd take this all terrain golf cart as it may an easier ride for you. We don't want you having that baby earlier, not because of my driving anyway," she chuckled lightly, smiled and drove off with just the two of them.

"I brought you a lemonade and me a beer, or two." She pointed. Kristan took the lemonade and sipped while Kate drove through the rows and rows of crops, sunflowers and hay.

"Do you have horses?"

"Yes, just a few, not too many. We grow their food, not grain, right here. We are going to add more flowers, especially lavender next year. And we are planting without all the fertilizers. We are trying just about anything we can. Doing our own studies, keeping the books."

"You say that Nancy came here eighteen months ago frail, thin and death seemed imminent." Kristan started the conversation wanting to know about Nancy.

"Yes, she had chemotherapy for breast cancer after mastectomy and now it was in her lungs and bones. Go figure. That sounds like a death sentence."

"Stage four I suppose. They call that living with cancer but it means eventual death. You just don't know the month." Kristan said.

"That's what they say. Who am I to question authorities? Though it seems like we almost kill people with drugs and surgeries, profits for you if you work in medicine with their loss of life, of hope, of living out peacefully until the good lord comes for you."

"And what do you owe her turn around to? Do you have an answer?"

"I don't. She had nowhere to go but up or death. So she got up every day, walked, drank lemonade with freshly squeezed lemon juice, ate fresh fruit and grilled meat every night. Maybe her therapy fixed her and the timing of giving up, coming here and letting the spirit of God through prayer all added up for recovery. She never looked back. She said she was dying doing all that chemo and she couldn't do anymore. That's why she came here. She said she felt like the chemo lowered her resistance making the cancer actually grow stronger and more aggressive in nature. She wanted to find a spot where her own body fought those cells. She wanted an equilibrium she hadn't had in quite a while. I believe she found that here. We'll see. Time will tell."

"I'm happy for her. She looks like a million bucks. Pretty, pink skin and always smiling."

"We are not going to boast miracles here. We want peace, tranquility and healthier outcomes, even if that is just a happy outcome for the little time they have left. After all, we are born, we must die. Let's smile and be kind in between."

"I like your philosophies. Maybe you are on to something, blending less medicine with happy living. The plantation or farm is quite a concept. It brings an expansive feeling, opportunity, freedom from worries by working and producing together."

"I'm glad you like it. And it is not just about cancer patients. We are helping young men achieve and work hard, those that have been in some trouble. We need the muscles to do the crops and barn work, etc. and they need to use the muscles given them towards a happy life. Many boys in that 16 to 22 years of age category are lost. They don't want their parent's philosophies and think their friends are the coolest while not feeling what direction to go into. Here we combine it all and the workout from a day on the farm usually rests their restless souls. The music relaxes the soul, the fire pit soothes the mind via the eyes and a good cookout nourishes the body."

She took her way back to the middle of the property where trees were planted in rows. "This here is the tree farm. It has pines and other saplings for the future. The bee hives are kept out here too. See over there. That's where our honey comes from." She continued driving, slowly, over the farm and back up to the front barn and fire pit. They walked inside the barn and there were the three horses in the stalls for the night. There was a few chickens cackling about and a couple of cats as well. They kept the hay in here to keep dry she supposed. Also the farm equipment was kept in the back as well. It was rather large. Kristan didn't know the first thing about farming but she suspected she could learn over a summer or two.

"Let's go look out near the back of the barn. Maybe a

few of the guys are getting some firewood ready for the pit."

Kate and Kristan walked through the barn to the back and through the back door. Once outside a couple of the guys were sitting on a bench holding more cats.

One stood up immediately, "Good afternoon Miss Kate." He turned to Kristan to recognize her.

"I'm Kristan," voiced Kristan.

"I'm Daniel, nice to meet you."

"And you as well."

The one sitting said, "I'm Chris, nice to meet you too!"

She smiled, "You, too." Kristan sat down and petted a cat. "You all have a lot of work to do around here. The farm work must take all day."

"There are slow months but summer here is about to get in full gear. Come back the end of summer and we'll have a break then."

"The end of summer?" she asked.

"Yes, at summer's end we can pace ourselves before the long winter. It all gets done eventually," said Daniel.

"Maybe I will come back at summer's end." She looked around. Maybe she would do just that.

Kate said they'd see them later and headed back for the golf cart to return to the house. It was time to bring the picnic outside. They loaded up plates, plastic wear, and cups along with food supplies. Tonight was hot dogs and hamburgers, potato salad, broccoli salad, fruit salad and yummy pies and strawberries, whip cream over angel cake. The new boys were cooking tonight testing out their grilling skills or lack of. Kate would help them if need be. Putting people right to work she found was the best recipe of all.

That night after dinner the instruments emerged and some of the guests played for the others. Harmonicas blending to two fiddles with an experienced guitar player set the background for the strong voice of Kate. This went on for a couple of hours with storytelling in between. Kristan helped clean up bringing in items to the kitchen. She and Nancy put away items in the fridge then wiped down tables. Towards the end of these tasks someone came in and said, "She's about to tell the story of Palmetto Stars. Have you heard it?"

"No."

"Then get outside as quick as possible."

"Anybody heard this story before?"

"Sure. Yes. Tell it anyway."

"Okay here goes...

Chapter 33). Swamp Story

"Eric, please tell our gentleman friend upstairs I wish to speak with witness A named Martha again. I have a couple questions for her, it will likely take thirty minutes or less before he brings down witness C the whistleblower."

"Sure thing," he said. He rose and ran lightly up the stairs to find the older man. He did. He was sitting on a chair out of site but in view once you were upstairs. Eric thought to himself, now there's a job for an older servant of the United States Air Force, or Army, Navy, Marines, helping out. Nice touch.

"Miss Kim, Martha is coming down to see you," the older gentleman called out.

Kim rose to meet her at the staircase and brought her back to the kitchen table.

They repeated the same procedure just like before.

"Martha, now that you've rested and collected your thoughts, I'd like to ask you a couple questions," Kim instructed.

"I'm here to help as much as possible. I hope it does some good. However, I'm sure there are much worse crimes out there like murder and rape, even illegal drug use or extortion, or explosions."

"Yes, everyone would say those are definite crimes. But we are also here to keep our civil liberties in this free society. And the internet poses some grave instances where liberties are at stake. From bullying to cybercrimes of theft, impersonation and beyond we want to stay on top, if not, ahead of this generational problem."

"Well said. Well said."

"Is there anything else, no matter how small or ludicrous it seems, that you want to say aloud? I know you are submitting other paperwork for the smaller items following this interview."

"Yes, this afternoon I was reminded of something, two things that bothered me. More targeting, I'm afraid."

"Go on."

"After I lived in another state, temporarily, I had to get new license plate tags, again as I had decided to not stay in that state after purchasing everything correctly. It was a pain. Just a pain, not to mention costly."

"Yes?"

"I went to the DMV right next to the sheriff's office, walked in, took a number, sat down and waited. When a lady became available I went to see how and what I needed to do for the transaction. She said I would need to bring something in that I didn't have with me and to return with the item. I said okay and went home to do this. I'm sorry I just can't remember what it was after doing this, moving, starting a business, then selling a house, moving again and taking care of my college kid's problems. It must have been a paper related to the car. I returned the next day. I thought I sure hope I get the same lady because she'd remember and I wouldn't have to tell the long story again. Once again this was about the title of my car being held by the bank and not a regular loan. I walked in and took a ticket, looked around, sat down and realized I'd have to wait as there were other people. She was busy and I just took the last ticket and all these people are waiting. Then, all of a sudden like magic, when her customer left my number was called-even though I was clearly not next in line. In fact, I didn't stand up right away thinking it was a mistake or something. I was called so I went to her happy my number was called. Just seemed like someone was controlling it, at a motor vehicle place, of all things or places. Funny. But the thing is that was so weird I didn't tell a soul. What would somebody think? They would think you are crazy and off your rocker. Made me think about our phones and computers and who controls them. But I had been to so many car registration places in one year it bothered me, especially the one in my small hometown. Are you ready? Here's the final weird one. It wasn't until I saw this in a movie I knew what finally happened. I knew this occurred to me but it was confirmed who could do it when I saw it in a movie."

"I'm so intrigued right now. I'm about to pee my pants- please tell me."

Witness A let out a laugh. She continued on, "My husband and I were going out to dinner one night, a place I had been before with a girlfriend, a neighbor, and even my daughters."

"Okay so a very public place."

"Local restaurant, New Orleans style place. By the time we drove down the street maybe about three or four miles, the power grid was out for that area. A small area but exclusive to that restaurant. We still parked and tried to walk in as there were patrons still inside. But then we left and went to another place. Because I felt stalked, traced, and targeted I thought what the heck? No. No it couldn't be. That's a coincidence. Right?ABsolutely Wrong. When I saw the movie and it was a well-known organization in the United States I said geezuz fuck Martha, you are in trouble. Big trouble. I was scared to death. I was wishing someone would be on this case like a journalist or something. I needed someone to save me from this."

Kim could see her hands were writhing, her voice was shaking and this bothered her. If this is true, this is malicious, vile and totally unacceptable. "Please finish. I believe you."

"Oh, thanks. I'm still waiting on that journalist to verify these visions of no accountability of someone, unless it's AI, or artificial intelligence. And actually, wow, if it's AI that can hurt somebody real bad. That there shit shouldn't be put on anyone. And a human did that. For the first time I felt I now knew how the mob gets to people to swing their vote or their verdict in a case. They fucking scare them to death and threaten the little guy. Like me."

Kim shook her head, which didn't go unnoticed by Martha.

"At first, I thought, the Chinese are the smartest so it's them. Then I even entertained that USA is behind it. Man. We better get up to speed. One kid I know was going to work at a startup delivering food, locally. They had their tee shirts, hats and drivers. The night before it was to start their web server crashed. Was this a bigger corporation stopping the little guy?"

"That's what I'm going to find out. I promise you to find out as much as possible. You know some things cannot be put out to the public, but I promise that justice will prevail because you are so brave. We must fight back for the little guy. We must."

Martha wanted to believe this but she remained skeptical of everything. Would she ever relax again?

"When do you think this started, like is there a point where things went bad?" Kim asked.

"Well. It had to be back in 2013. I noticed that my emails decreased and someone wrote the word PRISM on a blog post. I didn't understand it at the time, didn't seem important but people on the net disappeared from writing blogs and poetry sites. I looked it up cause you can google anything you don't know and it was something about the large dragnet of our phones, conversations, and internet spying. Something about going in the back door which I didn't understand at all. Maybe you will."

"I will try."

"For seven years now I have felt violated by the internet, 2010-2017. Why didn't I stop? Because I needed to write more books. And I have. But I haven't made any money so maybe I should have quit many moons ago."

Kim held her hands. She believed this woman with all her heart. With her training she felt this is about as close it gets to internet terrorism, targeted intimidation but based upon what? She had to find the reason beyond a brother in federal prison.

Next up, the whistleblower. Maybe the whistleblower would answer her question.

The whistleblower named John gave his statement and answered every question that was asked. Unfortunately, he verified everything Martha said. And more. He gave more instances, possibly a few things she forgot. This wasn't just the net, it was her phone and real life instances. Fuck. He couldn't speak about the case in front of the federal building but he gave a person who worked that specialty and maybe they could help with that one.

The older gentleman made dinner for all of them. The three witnesses ate upstairs separately. They would be removed tonight, separately. Eric, Kim and Ben ate together and Ben told them about the beautiful sunset on Lake Half Moon. Maybe they would like to go for a canoe ride tonight after dinner. They said they would. Ben said everything would be taken care of here and tonight the house would be empty except for the three of them. He thanked them for their service. They reciprocated.

Kim and Eric went for a slow canoe ride around the lake enjoying the setting sun. The sounds were light, winds calm allowing single canoe ripples on the serene setting. The heavy work was done for now. Kim relaxed. Eric brought them a bottle of wine and poured her a glass.

"Here, you deserve this. The day is over and a long one at that." She took the glass and sipped the red wine. She closed her eyes after the next sip and thought of nothing.

"I don't want to startle you, but, there's a snake wrapped on my paddle."

"Oh yeah. Please," she started to say.

"Seriously, take a look before I set him free."

She turned to see his empty paddle, but it wasn't. Just then a thrust of water splashed all over her but she held her gaze. An alligator came out of the water, took the snake and paddle with it. As quickly as it came out it went back in the water and took the snake wrapped paddle with it. The fight was in the water and the canoe couple watched but not for long.

"Kim, paddle, or better yet, give me your paddle and I'll get us back to the shore near the dock. He's got his dinner so he's not after us," he said with a smile.

"Get me out of here. Now!" she screamed. She startled the swamp. She wasn't sure she wanted to return here, ever. One night. What could possibly happen in one night? "But first, more wine. Please." She held out her glass and he poured her a full cup.

Ben made them dinner and they sat in the living room to eat. After dinner he poured them a Tennessee Whiskey and put some music on of the same name. These three souls in this room and the three upstairs were on the same page of seeking justice and the song just seemed to permeate the air with goodness.

By the time she laid her head on the softest pillow in all the world she couldn't think of anything. So she didn't. Except she said a prayer out loud for her companion named Kristan. She would see her tomorrow.

Eric slept just outside the bedroom on a couch near the fireplace. The night had ended well. No one was hurt in the swamp. He was prepared, of course, as he took his gun with him and he'd shoot. Hell yes, he'd shoot. People over animals, or reptile's, every day, if it had to be that way. He overheard her when she said a prayer for her traveling companion. How sweet. The lady had a big heart, smart mind and beautiful soul set with good intentions. Best to her. He fell asleep.

Ben made them breakfast in the morning. Then they left the swamp for good.

Chapter 34). Palmetto Stars Origin

Upon returning to the farm Kristan welcomed Kim back. They talked swamp stuff and made the plans for their departure on Monday morning. The drive wasn't long so no need to leave super early. They set it for 9 am with a stop for lunch on the way. Perfect. Kristan told Kim how she really liked this place and she'd been invited back. It was close to her school and she was entertaining the idea maybe even before school started. Kim commented that Kristan seemed to have grown overnight. Maybe the baby would come early she thought. It wasn't low yet so she still had time. She at least wanted to meet the parents to be before the birth to get a connection going.

"Here we are talking all about me. But you, you had the adventure! Please tell."

"I did many things in my training to be in the service for the United States. But swamps are not where I want to be. I just don't. I can handle climbing a mountain, walking for miles, even swimming in the ocean for a race or to escape a foe but alligators think I'm bait-so we are not good. They are like leftovers from the dinosaur age, I swear." Kim honestly explained her adventure. "However, the interviews went very well. I'm eager to source it to programmers and connect all the dots. We'll see."

"I hope you can help those ladies. Seems like it might be the tip of the iceberg since you are getting a commission, or task force, on it."

"Eric, my partner seems to think it may be a new agency but at first they'll keep it private so the big guns aren't alerted."

"Do you think there is a swamp in our Capitol?"

"Kristan, what a question? Wow, let's just say I didn't know we had one until a couple years ago. Very difficult to do business with people that want to undermine you. Our security services, men and women working for the armed forces are strong, honest people. But like anything there's always a bad apple or two. We want those gone. The rotten bunch of apples need to go."

"I applaud you for going into the services. I couldn't do it. I can't kill another human."

"Kristan, I think you could kill a bad one. You would never think twice about it. That person kills children, murders others, blows up buildings and wants to kill you. But, hopefully, we can stay out of wars, protect us at home and keep our borders secure. It is a big job."

"What degree are you looking to obtain?"

"I'm thinking of changing it from nursing to finance. Money is power and I'd like to be in on decision making plans that benefit and motivate others well-being. Miss Kate told me about the programs she's a part of behind the scenes."

"Maybe after the summer before school starts I'll stop

back and stay without this. Then she and I can talk more about my future."

"After we pack what's on the schedule today?"

"You can go for a run around the whole place at ten, gardening at eleven, lunch at twelve, yoga poolside at two and a nap at three o'clock, followed by badminton from four to six."

"Nap at three?'

"That's for me and the baby."

"Good one."

"I'll be doing gardening, lunch, pool, nap and badminton."

"I'll up you one and go for all of it. A run at ten sounds good."

Dinner was outside near the pool and fire pit. Tonight was skirt steak with peppers, onions, tomatoes and cheese with beans on the side and skewered melon. After dinner was s'mores and stories around the fire.

"Miss Kate, tell the story about how Palmetto Stars got its name," asked one of the newcomers.

"I meant to tell that last night but it got too late. Sure. It's actually not that long."

"Back in 1886, after the civil war, things were expanding everywhere across America. I think you could say it was a boom time for growth from shops, to printing presses, railroads, steamboats, and even bicycles, as people were moving around. Badminton was a game for fun and the ladies could play it as it was not rough. They could play it in their long dresses even though the hems had not yet risen.

My great-great-great grandmother was playing badminton over on the west side of Florida near a coastal hotel. She was visiting with friends from New York and Ohio. They had been riding bicycles all day and that evening before dark, or almost dark, they had a badminton match, a contest if you will. She loved the game and was quite good at it but I suppose the evening hour close to sunset, and mixed with some imbibing, caught her off guard. She lost her balance. She ran backwards to get a shot, tripped and fell. I guess she must have hit her head and passed out for a while. When she came back around to her senses she saw a sky full of stars surrounded by palmetto leaves. She'd stumbled into a palmetto bush and missed the shot. End of story." An applause of laughter settled down.

"What about the name?"

"Later on she started a small grocery store further down the coast. I think it's still open down in Florida. We decided to name this farm after her. She was so full of life enjoying everything she could get her hands on. She loved to travel and keep moving. She took stagecoaches, trains, horseback, automobiles and bicycles. Later on Multiple Sclerosis took her legs; she couldn't move them and had to use a cane, eventually a walker and finally a wheelchair. We celebrate her and her energy, spirit and sense of humor. Her picture is in the dining room-she's standing next to a bicycle. It's blown up. The end."

"Therefore we hold our badminton games today."

Later that night after the badminton games Kim sat with a few of the guys doing the hard work on the farm. One of the guys was the nephew to the owner. He told her she had really helped him during a low period of his life. He feels indebted to her in a good way. He also realizes he has more growing up to do. This young black gentleman really touched Kristan. They talked about poetry and college classes and her mom. Then she told him about her new friend in Savannah and didn't understand why God would introduce someone, and take them away so quickly after a wonderful yet brief encounter. She looked at this young man with light brown eyes waiting for an answer.

"I have an answer for you."

"You do?"

"Because God loves you so much, cares about what you're doing and where you're going, he put an angel in your path on her way to heaven." He looked away up to the stars, she took his hand and kissed it. Then she cried a storm.

Kim and Kristan left at nine and immediately stopped for coffee and a chicken biscuit with hot sauce and strawberry jam.

"Are you ready to meet them?" asked Kim.

"I am. I'm ready to have this baby. I hope they are ready. I talked with them a few days ago. Tomorrow we'll go to the doctor together. Today we have to get acquainted. I like the fact they are already parents. They know what to expect."

"When will you tell the birthfather?"

"The right time will happen. It hasn't hit me yet. Promise, you won't judge me?"

"Honey, you are one brave girl. Smart too. I won't judge you," replied Kim.

"I think after I go home I'll write a letter to him. I'll go to the big graduation party at the lake, see that he's okay and his plans have gone forward. I'll give him the letter to open when I'm not around. That way he can sort it out, he can see if he wants involvement or not. No pressure."

"Kristan, you are extremely thoughtful and full of such wisdom. No everyone possesses that quality but you do."

"I'll write that letter when I get home. For now it's me and the baby and the family to be."

Kim turned off the radio and set the cruise control. They drove on I-10 to their destination. The highway was quiet today with minimal traffic. There was no tension in the vehicle. Kristan took a nap but told Kim to wake her twenty minutes before arrival. She wanted to be fresh and wide awake. "Can we hit the bathroom before that too?"

"Sure thing."

"Great."

"Just so you know I will be talking business with James after we arrive, not at first, but after the appointment. I don't want you to think it's anything about you and the baby."

"It's about helping those girls and your mission. You go girl. I'm with you. Maybe I'll change my major. I thought the farm rocked," Kristan said and fell asleep.

Kim smiled and kept driving. Today was not a long trip, but held pretty scenery with ranches scattered here and there at times.

She woke her like instructed. Made a trip to a gas station for gas and a pee break.

They arrived about ten minutes later and pulled in the driveway of a white sided house with green shutters and a carport. She could see a large grassy area out back and it held a swing set. Two cars, one a truck the other a nice sports car was under the tin roof. Modest. Nice. Neighbors on each side in a community. The thought crept over her, her daughter would be living here, but she pushed it aside. Their daughter would be living here. The side door opened and a couple came out holding hands smiling and looking at the passengers seated inside. They didn't want to rush them and gave them a moment.

James came to Kristans side and opened her door. He held her hand to exit the car. Megan came around after saying hello to Kim and took Kristans hand from James. "I'm so glad you made it. Here we are. We are thrilled to finally meet you."

"Me too. Megan and James, well, I'm Kristan and here's the baby." She held her hand to her tummy making swirl motions.

"Let me get your bags and let's all go inside. The boys are with their grandma and grandpa letting us have some alone time to talk and learn about one another," James said.

"All the bags are in the back." They walked in to a very clean home nicely decorated and full of pictures of the family. Megan explained about her and James getting married a couple years back, then moving to the beach and opening a dive shop. They have two boats, one that takes out the divers and another they use for pleasure. They are so happy they made the move and the boys love it too. All the kids know how to swim and the oldest has gone diving once after he took a course.

They chatted for about an hour. "If you don't mind, Kristan and I, will go pick up the boys unless you need to rest, while James and Kim get caught up on work talk."

"Yes, I can go with you because I already took a nap today in the car. I need to walk around a little." The two drove off to pick up the boys.

Chapter 35). Birth of a Daughter

Three days after the doctor's appointment and several days of getting to know one another Kristan's water broke sitting outside one afternoon. James was at the shop but Megan was there and ready to assist. They called the doctor and timed her contractions. The doctor wanted her to go to the hospital. They had waiting rooms there and she felt certain this was going to be an easy or rather quick birth. Kim loaded up the suitcase for Kristan. She gave her a big hug.

"I'll do whatever I can to help you. Just order me around."

"Thanks. I do wish my mother was here but she and I talked. We decided that it would become more my family and not the baby's future. So hold my hand and keep me breathing."

"This doctor, I'm told, is excellent-she is all for the mother and baby and comfort for both."

"I'm getting an epidural. I mean why not? What do I want no modern medicine? I'll take it and a few pills later to get over the episiotomy."

"Sometimes, I've heard women don't even need them."

"It's amazing the whole process. This one lady told me she practically levitated over the bed and this big gush came out and there was the baby. It was a relief of joy she couldn't explain."

"I like that. I'll remember that someday when I get married and have children. That sounds almost divine or heavenly Miss Kristan."

"Okay, let's vamanos, aribe!"

Megan packed a few treats, or snacks, just in case things went longer. She also put her little four pack of champagne mini bottles in a lunch cooler-to celebrate in the room. She needed to get balloons and flowers, she must tell her husband to get those on the way to the hospital. She wished she was having the baby girl but this was super cool, a celebration of life and she didn't have to go through the labor of love. She cherished the thought of Miss Kristan and her brave contribution to complete her own family. Megan would hold her in her heart forever!

The hospital was fifteen minutes away and Kim drove very cautiously. She took her right to the emergency room door, unloaded the two of them, and then parked. Once inside she was instructed to the birthing rooms. There was a whole wing for this kind of thing. Each room was actually two rooms combined with a living space, birthing area and emergency set up if needed. It looked like a fancy modern hotel with curtains not hospital grays or greens but real color and artwork. Why not give birth here? Music was playing and a nurse was showing Kristan where to put her things and how to operate the place, call buttons, kitchen, music, etc.

"Thank you so much," Kristan said and went to get dressed in a hospital gown. The nurse wanted to evaluate where she was in her labor.

"You can wait right over there in the living room while I check her labor." She closed a sliding door that gave them privacy. Once James got here they could all be on the other side waiting for the arrival.

James came in with balloons and flowers he'd purchased on the way. The boys were at grandmas and grandpas house until tomorrow morning. He set them over in the corner as to not distract from the immediate center, Miss Kristan. "Where is the lovely mother to be?"

"She's behind curtain, or door number one," said Megan and pointed. "Come sit, I'm so excited. Are you?"

"Yes, I can't believe it's time already."

It would be the four of them today and tonight.

"Hello everyone." Kristan opened the door and waved. "She said we have some time so settle in. Check out the TV, music, and kitchen over there," Kristan pointed, admiring the place.

"I brought you and the baby some flowers and balloons to enjoy," James explained. "What can I get you right now? Or even later, if you feel like it, I'll run get whatever you want. Okay?"

"That sounds like a plan because I'm kind of hungry right

now."

"I can run out right now. Did she say what you can eat or not?"

"She said don't eat until the doctor gets here-she'll be here in thirty minutes."

"Okay here's what we'll do. Give me your order and when I see her arrive I'll run out and get the food so you don't starve," James kept busy writing her order down.

When he finished Kristan decided to take a walk in the hospital corridors and Megan went with her. "We'll stay on this floor because you never know when lightning strikes."

"Lightning strikes?"

"Two of my boys came fast, the first and the third, and the third came like lightning. He came out so fast there was no one to catch him, so my mom put her hands down there and cradled him until the doctor turned back around. The twins are like three minutes apart."

"Incredible. You are the mom," Kristan slapped her airborne palm against Megan's.

She put that hand on her hip and stopped walking. The women looked at one another.

"I think the baby is coming. I feel a need to push," whispered Kristan.

"I'm not your doctor but hold the push and let's return to the room. Right now."

Megan put her in the room, told Kim to watch her and she walked quickly to get the nurse. She returned with her and saw the distress on Kristan's face. Probably another contraction. She told them to time these and went to page the doctor who was in house as she had received that alert

The nurse came back and gave out a few instructions after asking about the contractions. The contractions were closer and birth would be imminent. She had her prepare to lay on the birthing bed and checked her cervix again. "The doctor will be here in a few minutes and then after she arrives you can push with the urge. Okay," said the nurse.

Kim and Megan were here. James, not realizing how close she was, went to get her food to eat once he knew the doctor was in house.

The epidural was inserted and Kristan was made comfortable on the birthing bed. About thirty minutes after the epidural all were present and Kristan was allowed to push. James made it back with her food and set it in the kitchen. He went up near her shoulders and held her hand from time to time. Labor was smooth, swift and revealed the crown, followed by the shoulders, body and legs. The nurse cleaned off the blood and spatter, wrapped the baby and set it up to the mother's arms. Kristan held her, looked at her, kissed her cheek and wept. Then she invited Megan to hold the baby with James for a few minutes. After a while the nurse took the baby over to a bassinet to do a second Apgar score. It was an eight. Everything seemed to be fine. The baby had all ten toes and fingers, color was pink and breathing was good. The heart rate was accelerated like a baby's is and the toes fanned out appropriately. The doctor would do an exam before she left but first the afterbirth and making sure her patient, the mother, was doing well enough.

"The baby can sleep in here with you tonight," said the nurse to Kristan and the others.

"Okay."

"Are you okay with that? We'll come and check on her a couple times and you can feed her too." The nurse instructed. Megan and Kristan had made the decision to switch back and forth with feedings for a few days. One could begin to bond, one could begin to let go, and then James would help once they were home. Kristan felt that by feeding her it would be fine, it was real and she was still comfortable with the outcome.

The next morning it was silent in the birthing suite but colorful. The flowers and balloons decorated the place while three women and a baby slept. James skirted out early to retrieve breakfast. He placed it at a table near the kitchen. He made coffee and a pitcher of mimosas. He set the table and poured the mimosas. Then he sat down and waited. He could hear some baby noises, he rose and went to the bassinet, and picked up the baby. He sat back down and held the baby wondering if it was time for feeding or changing. He wasn't sure but the baby wasn't crying so all was good. He looked at her cute little cheeks. Today they would go home and begin to be a family. He was extremely grateful for this moment and shed a tear down his own cheek. Then one by one the ladies rose and joined him at the table. A little later the nurse came and got the baby and took her to the nursery.

"I hope they don't mix her up with another baby," said Megan.

"That sounds like a true mother, afraid for her child, a momma bear instinct." Kim said matter-of-factly.

"They know what they're doing. I like this place. If, or I should say, when I have another baby I want to have it right here."

About an hour later they brought the baby back and discharged the patient and baby to home. "Mom needs to come back in three days with the baby," said the nurse. Here's formula and diapers and her records.

Megan said, "Thank you. Thank you very much for all you've done. I think I speak for everyone here."

"It used to be that the baby had to sit on a nurse's lap in the wheelchair to be discharged when adoption was involved but we changed our policy to be sensitive, in this case, for everyone involved. The adoptive mother may hold the baby in a wheelchair with a nurse pushing while the adoptive father wheels out the birth mother in a wheelchair to the car. In your case we involved everyone."

"Oh wonderful. You thought of everything."

"We aim to mainstream. Why not?" Kristan thought what a cool nurse. She was feeling like that was truly a sign from heaven, or maybe from Scarlet, in a divine way.

This adoption was a celebration of life. For all. Baby included.

Chapter 36). Brunch & Shopping

Five days after the birth of Amelia two moms set out to dine and shop that is to go to brunch followed by shopping at a few stores near the water. They went to Megan's favorite place Harbor Walk Village. And since it was Sunday Harry T's was open and serving brunch, champagne brunch that is.

The girls arrived at ten wearing sundresses, hats and sunglasses, along with festive summer high heeled sandals. A few hours by themselves would be heaven. Megan left the boys at home and the new baby. Kim and James were there and would handle everything. For Kristan she was baby less, or not pregnant, to put it bluntly. That alone was freeing to her. That thought elevated her spirits even more. She wasn't celebrating her mistake in life, as some might call it. The only mistake is the timing. Her celebration was for herself. She would not be bogged down with ill thoughts or worries the rest of her life if she had aborted. Someday she would see the child if all went well. That would be okay too. She felt like Megan would keep her in the loop and be available to her. So as not to confuse the child she would not be in her life on a daily basis but maybe a Christmas or two. She looked at Megan and this new mom seemed overjoyed like her cup spilled with plenty to go around.

The waiter sat them outside at table twenty three near the harbor where they could watch the boats come and go. He laid the menus down and said there's no rush ladies.

Will you be having champagne? And they both said yes!

"You look so happy Megan. That makes me happy." Kristan started.

"I didn't even know there was an emptiness, a gap, if you will. James and I married and my three kids came with that package. He loves them, seems to be a good dad as he's learning all the time. The boys like to play with him. He's hands on."

"I can see that. He's very physical and fun."

"He mentioned he would like to expand the family, maybe have our own children together and asked me how I felt. Of course, I love him and wanted him to experience the joy of being a parent with a new baby. Then you came along. Kim called and ran it by me and we both thought, that is the perfect gift. It felt right. I know you could have placed your baby with a hundred other couples and maybe they deserve that more than us. But I also felt like it was meant to be."

"I feel the same. Kim has helped me very much with my thoughts, decisions and showing me other ideas in life. I kind of figured God sent her there to enlighten me and take a chance. So, I followed through. Also, if you two were her friends y'all must be nice people."

"I like the idea you were from the same area as me. Maybe someday you'll stop by and say hello to my mom. Then again, it might make her sad."

"How about we handle holidays, or times and places to meet as we see them. No plans-just ask and never more than three times in one year. That might confuse the child. What do you think?"

"I like the idea of being open but you are right no more than three times in a year so we don't confuse. Letters and pictures will really help, I think. Can you send twice a year a big update with pics?"

"I will do that. Very easy to do through our phones or maybe I'll print out the good ones and send in a card."

"I like that idea. I'll look forward to seeing her enjoying her family."

They sipped their champagne and poured another glass. The view was out of this world.

"I see a plane flying all above the harbor. Must be a sightseeing tour."

"The boats are little busy bodies coming and going. They take people staying here at the hotel to an island over there and let them off to suntan, read books or snorkel offshore."

"Look there's a floating bar. Its round. And some of these yachts are humongous!" Kristan exclaimed.

"Let me take a picture of you, a couple pictures, and then you can remember what a fabulous place your daughter is growing up in." Megan instructed.

Kristan smiled, stood up and went to pose in front of all the activity. She turned side to side and lifted her head up raising her arms in a joyous moment. Megan snapped away.

"I'll take a picture of both of you if you'd like," said the waiter. The two wrapped their arms around each other and leaned in like they'd known each other a lifetime. A lifetime, after all, can be a few hours or days, or an eternity. Sometimes it's a light switch or a click of the fingers to gather attention. In this case it was life, the bond of a baby and the promise of a bright future.

Breakfast came. Megan ordered eggs, bacon and French toast while Kristan had crab cake eggs benedict with fried green tomatoes slathered in hollandaise sauce. Yum. The sun was bright but they were under cover wearing their sunglasses and smiles. Celebrating a new baby's birth eating brunch, sipping champagne and chatting with a new friend created a memory neither would forget. Both moms were feeling a joy in their heart bonded by a newborn named Amelia Elise.

The two mom's walked and walked after brunch and shopped a couple stores looking here and there. Mostly they passed time. A band was playing in a small theater stage right off the walkway. The music added to the festivities. This was a lively place with lots of fishing, eating, boating and people watching. Kristan didn't want to chance a boat ride yet being post-partum and Megan understood. Kristan bought a new sundress that she would wear to the summer party at the lake next month. Megan bought a nine month little onesie with a lighthouse on it.

"That's so cute. Adorable. That would be the fun part, all the dress up times and fixing of the hair. I guess I will have another baby someday. I never thought about all the great little things you get to do."

"My boys will likely quarrel over who gets to fix her hair. Lol."

"They'll teach her kickball, I'm sure."

Chapter 37). James and Kim Get Down To Business

The next day, the day before Kim and Kristan would head back to Atlanta, Kim and James met for a private meeting at an undisclosed location. He had a private little bunker out back unseen from the road. They would discuss their cases, check for coincidences, and report back to their agency. Megan had started to assist and learn the trade with James to finish up the business up north. They now ran a dive shop and would stop the undercover biz, or maybe return to it after the baby was older. He led her out back behind the car port and tall shrubs to a shed.

"I'm sorry to see you leave James, you're so good at what you do."

"Well, as you know, my family just recently grew and I'll devote more time in that capacity. But maybe after six months or so we'll come back, both of us working together."

Kim looked around. It was a comfortable little shack with a couch and yellow swivel office chair. "Megan picked that out. She thought the bright sunny color reminded her of pineapples. She thought it would lighten and brighten my day. And it does when I'm out here-about once a day."

"Okay, let's chat. My details from last weekend have been sent to the bosses. The witnesses seem credible and I feel like we did our part. We didn't ignore their voices. I'm good with that. I also hope the programmers figure out the rest so we live, we learn, we conquer injustices."

"Man, you make me want to re-enlist. I love that you are spot on. I wish you the best. And now, I have a little girl, I must help protect those vulnerable lives. And we are all vulnerable with these," James pulls out his phone.

"You go first. Go over the details of the bar explosion."

James looks right at her with his intense eyes, dark hair and skin, and says, "Nineteen eighty four, or nineteen hundred and eighty four dollars means nothing. We got side tracked on that. The dude paid the lunch tab with sixteen bucks, so he stiffed him from the two grand."

"Makes sense now. But the whole big brother thing seemed so in focus."

"The money amount is not a clue. The government CIA dude was a loner and paid him, the investigator, to surveil someone who was involved in a big case. What we didn't know was that he, the investigator, stole a gun from him, it was in the other pocket, and we are not sure how that ties in. The dude getting paid died, as initially we thought so, in the explosion out back, while the government loner walked away without the money or the gun. Makes us think someone else did the explosion confronting the loner, not to mention the dead guy."

"So have you found the explosive guy?"

"No. And here's the stinger. The guy out back didn't die; he's a protected witness."

"Then you'll be able to identify the government loner."

"Bingo. We already got him identified. But he didn't kill, or not kill, the guy out back."

"Where is he do you think?"

"Laying low but may come around when this big trial gets going come fall."

Kim asked, "What about the nice lady named Maria and her daughter Hope?"

"NSA did a dragnet, Maria got caught up in that with the link to Scarlet's nephew. The guys have been found and fired for causing havoc." James explained.

"The two guys on the lake with cop hats in the back of their vehicle that Megan saw from her door were on assignment. Undercover. What she saw was real."

"Oh, that one really freaked her out. She had wild ideas about those two. She thought she was in the movie "Deliverance." James remembered. "Now tell me about the federal building."

"The federal building is a real puzzle but the shooting may be an international money laundering scheme, and her husband was Involved but bad actors played on her condition getting her out of the house."

"Huge diversion making her look like the bad cookie." James shook his head.

"Martha had her health records stolen via the internet, spies using it to destroy her sanity. They hacked her computer, social Medias and texting capabilities. They turned her camera on, relentlessly, even in the bathtub. They listened and recorded every single conversation she had. They followed her like she was a criminal, repeatedly. The bad guys went through her social Medias doing malicious things to frighten and scare her. Not only on her phone, they tricked her when she was on vacation with her family using tactics of highly trained spies not just from the US. They even hooked up her emergency system in the car to listen to her car conversations. They'd spook her with pictures of places she'd been to or persons she had just seen. Like out of another dimension, or twilight zone."

James asks, "But why. What's the point?"

"Her brother went to jail for five years but before that they terrorized her using a PI, hired by a terror group, working for a powerful operative to silence families and victims of cases brought forth. People in high places do mighty things."

"That's the case you are relying upon the programmers and others to assist. Somehow we have to make the system more stable, phones need to be safer from prying eyes."

Kim adds, "That is my new assignment. They've hired some young graduates to assist me in cyber security, not just for the big cases, but for everyday people losing their identity to revenge or vengeance upon another's soul."

"Maybe after about a year when the baby is older, Megan and I could assist you in these matters. I think she'd like something like that," James concluded.

"Tell you what I'll call you in six months and ask if you're ready. We need responsible and trustworthy, and nonpolitical people are our side of justice."

James broke out his bottle and poured them a couple shots of top shelf bourbon. "To you and your work. Thank you."

Kim looked at a picture on the wall. It was of a large fishing boat and she recognized the two passengers. "That's you and Megan sitting there," she said.

"Indeed it is. When we were dating we came down here to fish and check out the place to see if we'd like to live here. That day we caught three king mackerel and a Mahi Mahi. She loved the fishing. That sealed the deal for me."

"Cool."

"See the picture of the fish?"

"Yes, I do."

"After I hung this on the wall she said the famous whistleblower looked as pale as this fish during his interview on TV. She didn't know the fish drains his color when caught. She made me think about things in a newer perspective. Like a revelation, this picture signifies the whistleblower and the three agencies doing bad things. I titled this picture 'Three King Mackerel and a Mahi Mahi.'"

"Sounds like a book title." She commented.

"I know right? We need whistleblowers, some are truthful and brave, others not so much, but correcting our mistakes is paramount because we are all human. Period."

"She's smart. I like her. Risk, common sense and a whole bunch of laws detour our path but we have to work with it."

"You know where we fit in?"

"In the picture?" Kim asked.

"Yes." James said.

"Let me guess, the three kings represent our agencies: the NSA, the FBI, and the CIA."

"Yup. We all got caught. Someone turned us in, though, and that is actually a good thing." James relented.

"Except only a few were bad or harmful." Kim explained.

"That we know of." Paused James.

"Here we thought the money was the main clue but it was just a dumb fuckery. And most of you guys were not harmful like some. The bad apples needed to go, not good for the pie, you know."

"You're funny. Did you ever read the George Orwell book?" James asked.

"No, I haven't but I'm thinking it needs to be on my TBR pile." Kim mused.

He poured a second shot. He handed her the glass. "Sip on this one. To big brother watching big brother." Kim and James smiled close lipped and toasted one another.

Chapter 38). Goodbye

Maybe the downturn would come later or maybe it never would. Kristan felt sure that she would never have doubts, ever. Packed and ready to go they climbed in Kim's SUV and rolled down the windows after giving hugs to everyone.

"Kristan, we would understand if in a month or two you just had to come back and give her a hug. We really would," said Megan. "And if you get the blues please call me, okay?"

"Okay. Thanks."

"We are ready to go. It's a long trip about six hours," said Kim. She pulled away and they waved goodbye. James was holding the newborn Amelia Elise. They could see her little face and arms up in the air stretching.

She honked the horn and they were off. Neither spoke for a good half hour. Kristan suffered a tear or two but then she was dry. She turned on the music and drowned out any thoughts or mild boredom. Next up was her new life. Time to get thinking of all that was to come.

She plugged in her phone. During this whole week, except for the brunch and shopping, she'd kept it off and not charged up. She just didn't want to dote over pictures. She had a couple of her and the baby, which Megan had taken, and that was all she wanted. She would show her mother and father. After it was charged up she'd check on the details for the summer party at the lake.

Somewhere in the middle of Alabama where the highway was clean and neat and trees surrounded a lake next to the highway Kristan called Levi. Immediately she was thankful she did.

"Oh Kristan, I've been worried about you. I'm not on social media as class work took up so much time. How are you?"

"I'm fine. Thanks for thinking about me and wondering. Do you have time to talk?"

"Yes. Yes. Go on. Tell me everything. Then I'll fill you in on me."

She filled him in on everything. The last time she had

talked to him was before Scarlet got sick, back when all was okay-last winter. She started there with the sad affair, the funeral and moved on to the farm, and finally, the birth at the new parents place.

"What did you name her?"

"We chose it together. Her name is Amelia Elise."

"That is just beautiful."

"She is normal, no problems?"

"Yes, normal. I actually had it quite easy, it happened very quickly and rather painless."

"Yippee. Because I didn't want you to experience pain," said Levi.

"What a nice thing to say. I love that."

"I heard from your uncles the other day. After all we are cousins now, you know. They want me to come back to their castle on the east coast."

"Are you going to go?"

"Why don't you come with me? That would be more fun. You're not pregnant anymore-look how quickly that ended and gifting such a blessing to others. You are the bomb," Levi rattled on.

"I will think about it. When?"

"My summer job ends the last week of July, so maybe 1st week in August, or second week."

"Either week works for me. I'm going to head south afte the summer party up here and go back to this cool farm where they grow everything naturally. No cides."

"How long you staying there?"

"About a week or two."

"Let's make it the second week, that way if your plans get extended then we'll be fine. It will be a great sendoff from their place back to school."

"I totally agree," Kristan said. Kristan looked over at Kim She smiled. That smile that means, you got this girl you're doing fine.

Then she called her friend from high school to let her know she'd be home and wanted to go to the lake, the pool, and maybe a couple parties. Kristan would not be working this summer due to her circumstances and recovery time. She planned on exercising as soon as possible. She also thought about doing a summer abroad. Didn't that sound grand, mix in European travel with work, separated by language and cultures? Next summer.

"Kim, did you ever study abroad?"

"No, I did not. But when I went into the military I was

deployed to several countries over several years. I love Germany. It's beyond beautiful with castles and old towns. The people are friendly and it helps I like beer."

"I want to go to Ireland someday and maybe Paris. My mom lived there you know."

"No, I didn't know that. Well that is where you should go. You would have that in common and you could share memories."

"I like that idea." Suddenly everything was new, bright and beautiful. It helped she was with a very positive person. This lady wants to get things done. She's an accomplished person who checks off her list. Kristan thought when she got home she was going to snuggle with her mom for a few days, eat in pizza, etc., and then make her to do list in life and get on with it. No more boyfriends for a while, except friendship. She had Levi and Jeremy, some girlfriends and maybe some new friends at the farm. All was good. She would go to a gym for a month before the summer bash and then return to college.

Kristan and her mom spent several days cooking and watching TV. They caught up on shows, told jokes and made her dad some special dishes settling in the dining room to eat.

She showed her mom the pictures and went through every detail about the pregnancy and birth. Then her mom, Chloe, told her about her birth. They compared details and experiences.

"Someday, I'll do it again. I'll be a mom and love it to death, after I meet the right person," Kristan gushed. "But now I live just for me. Just. For. Me."

"She hugged her daughter, "You made many people happy by your decision: the baby, the mother, the father, three brothers, numerous grandparents, your dad and I, and most importantly you. You are brave, honest and a joy. I'm proud to be your mom. You make me look good."

"Thanks, mom. I feel good about it. But I don't put people down who decide the other way. I just want girls to know it's a wonderful choice with a happy ending. I'm glad I could participate in that, in making that family complete."

"Now you can help others because you've been through it yourself."

Kristan looked at her mom after she said this. She was right. She had done it. She could help in this manner, she could persuade.

Chapter 39). The Summer Party at the Lake

"It's by invitation only. Here's your invitation, Kristan." Kristan's best friend from high school hand delivered her invite and the two then went to lunch.

"What's the dress code? Is there one?"

"Dress nice, bring your bathing suit and change of clothes for the bonfire later on." Brittany was a full bodied young woman who thought she knew where she was going in life. She drew up plans and then fulfilled them, over and over. Would she ever really relax? Probably not. She was destined to deliver supervision and become the boss. Just like her dad.

"Are you planning it all yourself, or are your parents helping?"

"My parents are doing the food and I've hired the DJ so we can dance. We have the pool, the yard and the lake-so there's plenty of room. Only we girls will be allowed inside to change. There's an outside bathroom for everyone else to use. We should have some games though, right?"

"I'm terrible at games."

"Oh let's just do those corn hole thingy's."

"Perfect idea. I think you can rent or maybe some of the guys have them."

"We are going to have a couple tents to put the food under and a third one just in case it rains. My parents hired two lifeguards for safety and they won't tolerate wild play of any kind."

"Good idea. Then you don't have to worry about the crazies. What time is it over?"

"I forget. What time did I put on the invitation?"

"Ah... it says Summer Lake Party 5 PM until 10 PM."

"Some kids have midnight curfews because of their age. I think after 17 or 18 it's later. People driving can be home well before midnight. My parents wanted everyone to be safe and not causing havoc after hours. Do you want to stay over?"

"Because it's the party and you will have plenty going on I think not. But can I change my mind? I'll bring things just in case."

"Take a look here's some of the songs I'm going to have the DJ spin."

Kristan went home and wrote the letter for Noah. She wanted to get it out on paper, put it in an envelope and forget about it until the party. In life she knew you couldn't please everyone all of the time. But please yourself most of the time was her mother's motto and she borrowed it from time to time. This was the right time. She prayed about it and thanked God for giving her the strength and love to feel comfortable in her decision.

Kristan's mom helped her to find a party dress in her own closet. She had some gorgeous dresses as she had traveled back to Paris last November. She pulled out the short party dresses and laid them on her bed while Kristan picked them up one by one and held them up in front of the mirror. She narrowed it down to two and tried both of them on. One was black and ultra-sleek. Very nice. Then she tried on the floral Parisian swirl dress with spaghetti straps. Yes. This would be the one. She looked stunning in it. Her mom agreed. She'd wear her own heels and purse.

"Thanks mom. I love it. I feel like I should be strolling the avenues of Paris sipping a latte or something." Just then Kristan remembered she had bought a dress in Destin. Oh well, she'd wear it on the farm or at her uncles castle.

"It's perfect. I think you should wrap your hair up, sweep it up and back. Later take it down after you go swimming."

"Yes. She's having a photographer there to take pictures when we first arrive." Kristan floated her arms in the air and swirled about. Fun. It would be a fun night. "I better get going."

"Are you driving there?"

"I think so. I could take an Uber but I don't think I'm drinking."

"We could pick you up if you like. You might want to celebrate with Brittany as it is her graduation party from college. Didn't she ask you to stay overnight?"

"Yeah. Maybe I should. Ok. Maybe I will stay and you can get me in the morning. Perfect. Got to go."

Kristan poured herself a White Claw, her mom drank those, too. She prepped in the bathroom with makeup and curls in her hair that she swept up and back, then dressed.

Amazingly, she was recuperated from giving birth. Must be her young age she thought. Or maybe the small workouts were helping. Her tummy was practically flat. It wasn't that she didn't want anyone to know. She felt it her private business and she hadn't told the birth father yet. She had a small moment of doubt that maybe she should have told him. He did have a right, likely. But he was just getting going, hadn't even left for college or the air force yet. He'll forgive me. He has to understand. She thought she knew him and that he would.

She arrived at ten to five as Brittany wanted her there to greet the guests alongside her.

"Brittany," she said and hugged her friend.

"Kristan, come in. Say hi to my folks and we'll go out back. The photographer is setting up near the garden and pergola. Let's be first to get our pictures."

"You look great. I love your red dress and who did your hair?"

"My mom did my hair and I bought this dress online. Sweet, huh?"

"You do red. Sexy gurl!"

The two walked out back through the kitchen door to the patio. The grandness of the back yard was spectacular. Kristan reminded herself that Brittany lived in a mansion on the lake, the biggest house of anyone she knew with an expansive backyard filled with two pools, terraces, gardens and a lawn that stretched to the lake. Brittany was privileged but didn't act it. Her dad was probably the richest guy in town. She could see cars pulling in to park way over down the drive to the lake. The guests would be arriving up to the pool soon.

"Let's go down over here and get our picture taken-then we'll greet everyone."

"I'm right beside you." Kristan said and right there she decided to stay the night and tell her friend later after all the guests departed. Brittany would likely be thrilled she was spending the night.

The two young ladies posed for the photographer, laughing, smiling in sexy ways.

"Great. You all are beautiful and congratulations Brittany. Very proud of you." The photographer was a family friend.

"Okay let's go out to the pool."

The large pool in the center flowed into the lower pool and was surrounded by terraces, walkways and places to sit. The DJ was set up near the main pool where a makeshift dance floor existed. The two tents were off to one side and held the food. A cook and server were already starting up the grill getting ready to cook burgers and dogs.

The cars rolled in and guests arrived as couples and singles. Brittany had invited a hundred people, all of them friends and their guests. The music cranked up and the party was started. No one lived like this. Everyone had a smile knowing this was special. How nice that she was having a big summer party. Those that don't get to experience or live like this, which was practically everyone, get to for an evening. Nice treat. The guests kept their manners in check for now.

The areas around the pool were filling up with guests, mostly junior and senior college students, all friends of Brittany. Brittany was well liked in high school becoming president of her class and performing in the school musicals. Brittany and Kristan became besties when their mothers took them to lunch one day a very long time ago. Since then they've had sleepovers over the years, too many to count.

Brittany went around with Kristan at her side visiting and talking with her friends from over the years. She heard lots of congratulations about her degree. She had obtained a degree in film studies for the arts, a Bachelor's Degree in the Arts. She hoped to become a film maker centered in Georgia.

"Kristan, let's get some food and sit down for a bit." They poured a White Claw in a solo cup, made a plate of food and went to a nearby table set up for the party.

"Oh this is so good. Cheers." She toasted her friend and

added, "I have a gift for you and I'm staying overnight. I'll give it to you then. PS-I have something very important to tell you since you are my bestie."

"Perfect. That will be a surprise tonight. Can't wait!"

She high fived her.

Around eight o'clock guests started dancing to the DJ's music. Most had eaten and this was the next thing to do. It was still light outside. The fireworks would go off at nine o'clock over the lake from the water's edge. A few party goers were sitting on the dock drinking their light beer from a can. After a few dances Kristan went to sit down and just watch for a while. On her way to the garden table she ran into her old boyfriend Noah and his guest.

"Hello, Kristan. How's it going? Nice to see you."

"Hey, Noah. Good to see you too."

"Hi," said his guest. "I'm Merritt." She put her hand out to shake Kristan's hand. For some reason Kristan looked at her other hand. She didn't mean to but she did. Quickly, she looked away and up to her face. She returned the smile that came her way.

"Kristan. Noah and I are friends," said Kristan.

"Actually, we were boyfriend and girlfriend last year. Now we're friends," Noah just had to be honest. Kristan smiled thinking about the letter in her purse. She must give it to him before he leaves tonight.

"I'm glad we can be friends and nice to meet you. Are you staying for the fireworks?"

"Yes, we are. We are leaving after that," said Noah.

"Great. I have something for you-so I'll give it to you then."

"Sure. I'll look for you," said Noah. He and Merritt walked away towards the food tent.

Kristan wasn't sure and didn't want to act boldly but she thought for sure she saw an engagement ring on her other hand's ring finger. She would find out later. Her head swooned in a light kind of dizzying fashion. Really she thought. Oh boy. Kristan went to find other girls she knew in high school. She wanted to catch up on their freshman year and how it went for them. Many things are on Instagram and other social Medias but to get the real juice she wanted to ask first hand. You know chat. She pretty much stayed off Snap Chat and Tik Tok due to her condition. Come to think of it her friends probably felt like she dropped off the face of the earth. She was just going to tell them she had a chance to do a work study program in another city and went for it. Small white lie. That was okay because it was no one's business. When she finished college she could tell anyone, the world, but for now she wanted to keep her business private. She felt that was the best chance of success for all involved. She hoped Noah felt the same. She was almost certain he would.

Nine o'clock came and partyers were either swimming in

the pool, or the lake, while the fireworks got started. Kristan was doing neither. She'd go swimming tonight with Brittany after everyone left. She was happy just not that happy at the moment. She had a task and after that all would be well. She met Brittany at the cake table. Flowers adorned the cake as did the words: Congratulations Brittany! You did it!

"I'll take a vanilla piece please," she said.

"Here's the champagne that goes with the cake," said the server. Kristan and Brittany headed to a table with their glass of champagne and a slice of cake. She set her piece down and glass of bubbly when she noticed Noah and Merritt walking away from the cake table.

"I'll be right back. Give me two minutes." She picked up her purse and walked towards Noah. He stood up to greet Kristan.

"Kristan, you have something for me?"

"I do." She pulled out the letter and folded the envelope so he could fit it in his jean pocket.

"A letter?"

"Noah. I really care about you and am thrilled you got into the air force academy. I hope your future is as bright as it seems today," she said.

"Thank you. Why a letter?"

"I want you to read this when you are alone, spend some time keeping an open heart. It's a good luck letter with some thoughts from me. I'm happy we met and cared for each other," she said.

"I am too. I also have something to tell you." He paused. "Merritt and I are engaged to be married. She's moving out there with me. Obviously it won't be for a while but we fee committed to each other."

"I thought maybe I saw a ring wasn't sure though."

"Yeah. We are going to announce it in September over Labor Day."

"Then congratulations to both of you. Please read the letter alone, it's just for you. Thank you for being in my life." She hugged him and waved goodbye. He put the letter in his pocket.

Chapter 40). Palmetto Stars

Most of the guests were gone by 11:30. At midnight Kristan and Brittany went for a swim. By then they were all alone. They sipped their Claw from earlier and swam in the pool. The music was still playing just turned way down. Her parents were sitting outside on a chaise lounge listening to the music and enjoying their daughter's initial success due to graduation.

"Brittany, let's get another glass of champagne. I have

something very important to tell you."

Kristan went and walked to the cake table and poured another glass of champagne. Then she returned to the pool and got back in. She handed her friend a glass. "I want to toast you again. You got your degree in three years. Who does that?"

"Thank you. I know, right?! It helped by obtaining a whole year while still in high school. Then a couple fulltime summers and whoop, there it is!" Clink, clink. Brittany laughed and took a sip. She was enjoying the company of her friend. She had worked so hard, now she just wanted a month or two of fun.

"Cheers. I have to tell you something. Please don't be mad I didn't share before now but I didn't tell anyone. No one."

"Okay. I won't be mad."

"I went to Savanna because I was pregnant. Noah and I had spent a weekend together back in the fall. I decided to have the baby but not be its mother. I made a plan and placed the baby into a loving family in Florida. I haven't told Noah but wrote him a letter. He's happy and his life is moving forward. He's engaged to be married."

"Kristan. Whaaaaaaat?"

"I was pregnant. Had a baby. Placed it for adoption and here I am."

"Yes. I heard all that. Wow. You are incredible. Oh my God. Bless you," Brittany gushed.

"Just know if I could have told you I would have but I wanted to do it my way because it happened to me."

"I thought men have rights. Do they or don't they?"

"I think that's if they know about it, then they must be included."

"Well, babies are important. Do you feel bad about the decision? Like maybe you'll regret it someday?"

"No. I don't. Someday I'll have children. But if I never do, the family will allow me to be a small part of them. We talked it all out."

"High five girlfriend. Noah is really level headed I think he'll feel good about your decision." Brittany kept shaking her head and looking at her girlfriend trying to take it all in. It was incredible she kept it all to herself.

The friends finished their champagne and life just stepped up two notches. They had progressed to the inevitable that time marches forward.

A week later Kristan prepared to leave for college again, just like last summer, only now she seemed more grown up because life had forced her to make decisions that were life altering and altered the future. It would all be okay. She thought of the Scarlet she had lost in Savanna and the other one she'd briefly met down in South Georgia at a farm. She'd texted Kate and asked if she could stop by to see the place again on her way back to college. Of course, and please stay awhile if you can she said, adding, she couldn't wait to see her.

Her father had bought her a car for this year and she loaded up her luggage and things for the return. She hugged them and said goodbye, "Come and visit whenever you want. The house we've rented has an extra room or two for guests."

"We will," said her mother. "I'll let you know when. Have a nice time at your uncles, too, before you move in the house."

"Oh, I can't wait to see them. Jeremy and I will have a good time visiting."

She drove off and headed for the highway that led down south. Music playing. Thinking of the two places she'd visit on the way and whatever other ventures lay in store for her. Life was good.

She made it by dinnertime to the Palmetto Stars Plantation and was greeted by Kate. The forever warm and friendly second mom to many. A few were in the kitchen cooking up something delicious. Kate served her a lemonade. "Would you like something stronger?"

"Maybe later. Thanks."

"Miss Sarah Callais, or rather Scarlet, arrives tonight after dinner. She wants to see you and talk some."

"I do as well. Great."

After dinner Scarlet and Kristan talked in the front room which contained the piano and several settees to sit on. They discussed their lives, her projects, Kristans college and the pregnancy, and what lay ahead in her future. Scarlet said she'd like to keep in contact and check in on her progress from time to time. Kristan said she could come back here and either help out or visit from time to time. It was settled. That would happen. They got along fabulously sharing this very personal information. Then Scarlet said I would like to play and sing for you. Kristan was thrilled. It would attract others in to listen as well.

Scarlet was again dressed up as if she was ever ready to perform. Always on stage one might think. Kristan poured herself some red wine, a cabernet, and sat transfixed into another world. Scarlet played and sang for a couple hours to a full house. Music fills the soul like a bouquet entertains the senses, both send you to a place outside yourself.

The End

Epilogue

Noah opened his letter a week later in the privacy of his room.

Dear Noah,

I'm so glad I met you and we dated. I loved you and loved being around you. I know we said goodbye and that's okay. We are both going to have great lives, maybe because we shared ourselves with each other. Truly our time at the coast will live on forever.

Please keep reading and with a full heart understand I did this for both of us. I kept you in mind but in the end had a life decision to make-so I made it. I became pregnant from our time together after we had ended our relationship. We made a love child, if you will, but I didn't see us together and we both still were in search of our future. I could have ended it by having an abortion. Simple as that. Over and done with. No one would ever know, except me. Only a few seconds did I give this any thought. It was me. I would be all by myself.

I decided I would move to Savannah. My mom and I discussed the situation. I would be away from prying eyes and questions and stay off the internet for a semester, do a work study, deliver and place the baby for adoption. I realized this excluded you from participating. But remember, I could have just ended it. I found some wonderful people that helped me and the whole thing just fell into place.

I gave birth in Florida and met the couple whom adopted our little girl. We named her Amelia Elise. They have three boys, a family business and are wonderful people. I stayed with them for a couple weeks. Both of us can be present from time to time in her life. When you take all this in and are able to accept the situation I'll send you a picture and we'll talk further.

It is my hope you feel blessed by this decision. It wasn't a cake walk-yet, it felt absolutely the right thing to do. I don't condemn women who feel they have no choice but to abort. I just know for me ... I gave life to our love child, and in the end, made a beautiful family very happy. Now we can continue the life, our own lives, set before us.

Thank you for understanding. Much love and friendship. Be best.

Sincerely,

Kristan

And he did understand as he sat weeping holding the letter looking out at the beautiful blue sky.

www.ingramcontent.com/pod-product-compliance
Lightning Source LLC
Chambersburg PA
CBHW071342290426
44108CB00014B/1415